60
DAYS OF
PROPHECIES

60

DAYS OF PROPHECIES

THE TRUTH BEHIND END-TIME WARNINGS

DR. DAVID JEREMIAH

W PUBLISHING GROUP

AN IMPRINT OF THOMAS NELSON

ISBN 978-1-4003-4258-7 (audiobook)
ISBN 978-1-4003-4253-2 (ePub)
ISBN 978-1-4003-4250-1 (TP)

Library of Congress Cataloging-in-Publication Data

ISBN 978-1-400342501

Printed in the United States of America

25 26 27 28 29 LBC 5 4 3 2 1

CONTENTS

INTRODUCTION

"If Only I Had Known . . ."

Can you remember thinking those words during some of the more painful moments in your life? Even saying them out loud? Maybe you put off getting those physical checkups or tests your doctor (or maybe your spouse) kept mentioning year after year after year. Then, when you finally keep the appointment, the test results are painful. "If only I had known."

Maybe you never gave much thought to retirement or investment accounts during your working career. You had enough to think about each day without borrowing trouble from tomorrow. But then retirement came, and you had to figure out how to support yourself (and maybe continue supporting your family) without a regular salary. "If only I had known."

Or maybe you've had a friend or family member drift into the dangerous waters of self-harm or suicide. They never talked openly about their depression, but the signs became clearer once you saw them in the mirror called hindsight. You would have reached out if you'd been aware of what they were thinking and feeling. You would have helped. You *could* have helped. "If only I had known."

One of the universal realities among human beings is our confinement to the present. We can study the past and learn lessons from those who came before us. We can take an active interest in the present and observe quite a lot about what's currently happening. But we can't see the future. We can't know anything for certain about what's to come, and there's very little we can even predict accurately based on our current knowledge.

That's why the Bible is such an incredible gift. Yes, God's Word offers a record of history, including key insights about God's nature and character. Yes, Scripture offers much value in our present lives, including wise principles for living in alignment with God's will.

But the Bible also opens a window to the future. It shows us not just what *can* be, but what *will* be. It reveals what will happen during the most critical phase of human history—the phase we often refer to as the "end times."

This is the marvelous treasure chest we call biblical prophecy. Scattered throughout the pages of God's Word like veins in a mine are glimpses, visions, and promises of what God has planned for the end of this age—and beyond. And because these promises come from God, rather than from humanity, we can count on them. We can use them as a firm foundation as we navigate both current events and events to come.

While we often think of biblical prophecy as a New Testament phenomenon, particularly connected with the book of Revelation, the majority of prophetic passages are actually found in the Old Testament. We're going to take a deeper look at many of those passages in these pages. We'll also explore key portions of Revelation and other New Testament prophecies.

Don't let your life be defined by the regret of "If only I had known." Use these next sixty days to learn more about who God is and what He has in store for our world. Let's work together to mine the lode of biblical prophecy so that we can *know* what's coming—and so that we can approach the future not with fear, but with confidence.

ISRAEL REBORN

Prophetic Connection: *"For behold, the days are coming,"
says the Lord, "that I will bring back from captivity My people
Israel and Judah," says the Lord. "And I will cause them to
return to the land that I gave to their fathers, and they shall
possess it" (Jeremiah 30:3).*

May 14, 1948, was a pivotal day in human history. On
that afternoon, a car carrying prominent Jewish leader
David Ben-Gurion rushed down Rothschild Boulevard in Tel
Aviv, Israel, and stopped in front of the Tel Aviv Art Museum.
Four o'clock was only minutes away, and inside, more than
four hundred people—Jewish religious and political leaders
and press representatives from all over the world—were
assembled in an auditorium, anxiously awaiting his arrival.
Ben-Gurion quickly bounded up the steps. Precisely at four
o'clock local time, he stepped to the podium, called the
meeting to order, and read these historic words:[1]

> This right is the natural right of the Jewish people to be
> masters of their own fate, like all other nations, in their own
> sovereign State. Accordingly, we . . . are here assembled . . .
> and by virtue of our natural and historic right, and on the

strength of the resolution of the General Assembly of the United Nations, hereby declare the establishment of the Jewish State in Eretz-Israel, to be known as the State of Israel.[2]

Six thousand miles away, President Truman sat in the Oval Office, reading a forty-word statement about to be released to the press. He penciled in a few added words, then signed his approval and noted the time. It was 6:10 P.M. One minute later, the White House press secretary read the release to the world. The United States had officially recognized the birth of the modern nation of Israel.

Isaiah's prophecy, written 740 years before the birth of Jesus, declared: "Who has heard such a thing? Who has seen such things? Shall the earth be made to give birth in one day? Or shall a nation be born at once?" (Isaiah 66:8). Secular Israel was born that day.

The return of the Jews to Israel in 1948 was an astounding event unprecedented in world history. Never had a decimated ancient people managed to retain their individual identity through almost twenty centuries and reestablish their nation in their original homeland. The event was specifically prophesied, and it happened exactly as foretold. It was clearly a miraculous act of God.

REMEMBER: Despite long passages of time and unexpected obstacles, God is faithful to fulfill His promises. You can trust Him even when things seem uncertain.

GOD'S COVENANT WITH ABRAHAM

Prophetic Connection: *God made four vital promises to Abraham regarding the nation of Israel. We can see from history (and the present day) how those prophecies were fulfilled.*

The story of Israel begins in the book of Genesis. The very proportion of the coverage tells us something about the importance of Israel. Only two chapters are given to the whole story of creation. One chapter records the fall of man. Eight chapters cover the thousands of years from creation to the time of Abram. Then we find thirty-eight chapters that deal with the life stories of Abraham, Isaac, and Jacob—the progenitors of the Jewish race. Apparently, God finds Abraham and his descendants to be of enormous importance.

The Almighty God of heaven and earth made a binding covenant with Abraham, who was to be the father of the Jewish nation. The provisions of that covenant are recorded in Genesis 12:1–3. When you read that passage, you'll notice that God's covenant with Abraham consists of four unconditional promises.

First, God promised to bless Abraham. For thousands of years, the very name of Abraham has been revered by

Jews, Christians, and Muslims alike—a significant portion of the world's population.

Second, God promised to bring out of Abraham a great nation. Today more than 7 million Jews live in Israel, 7.5 million live in the U.S., and a significant Jewish population isscattered throughout the rest of the world.

Third, God promised to make Abraham a blessing to many. Just think what the world would be missing had it not been for the Jews. Without the Jews, we would have no Bible. Without the Jews, there would be no Ten Commandments, the Law that has largely been the basis of jurisprudence and statutory proceedings among most of the civilized nations of the world. Without the Jews, there would have been no Jesus. Without the Jewish Jesus, there would be no Christianity.

Fourth, God promised to bless those who bless Israel and curse those who curse her. No nation has blessed Israel like the United States of America, and no nation has been as blessed as the United States.

God has certainly kept his promises to Abraham. He has blessed him and the nation that came from him; He has multiplied his seed as the sands of the earth and stars of the sky; He has made him a blessing to the whole world; those who have blessed him have been blessed, and those who have cursed him have been cursed.

REMEMBER: Because God has been faithful to keep His ancient promises to Abraham, we can know that every promise will be fulfilled in Christ.

GOD'S CHOSEN PEOPLE

Prophetic Connection: *The tiny nation of Israel has played a major role in human history for thousands of years—and will continue to do so until the end of this age.*

When I first began studying prophecy, I remember reading an offbeat little rhyme about Israel by British journalist William Norman Ewer: "How odd of God to choose the Jews." When you think about it, this poetic quip expresses a valid observation. Doesn't it seem a little odd that of all the people on earth, God selected these particular people to be His chosen nation? Why would God choose the Jews?

We read about God's choice of the Jews in Deuteronomy 7:6, where He declared the people of Israel holy, chosen to be "a people for Himself, a special treasure above all the peoples on the face of the earth." The Bible tells us that His choice of Israel had nothing to do with merit. It was not because she was more numerous than other people in the world; she was the least (Deuteronomy 7:7). It was not because Israel was more sensitive to God than other nations. Although God called her by name, Israel did not know Him (Isaiah 45:4). It was not because Israel was more righteous than other nations. When God later confirmed His promise of land to the Jews, He reminded them that they were a rebellious, stiff-necked people (Deuteronomy 9:6–7).

If God chose to bless the nation of Israel not because she was more populous or spiritually responsive or righteous than other nations, just why did He choose the Jews? The answer: because it was His sovereign purpose to do so. His sovereign purpose means He cares what happens to His people and their land. He is not merely a passive observer to all that is taking place in Israel. As He told the people through Moses, theirs was "a land for which the LORD your God cares; the eyes of the LORD your God are always on it, from the beginning of the year to the very end of the year" (Deuteronomy 11:12).

REMEMBER: Israel has always been central to the story of redemption. As the world draws near to the end times, Israel will continue to play an important part in God's plans.

GOD'S PROMISED LAND

Prophetic Connection: *The Jewish people have never occupied the full boundaries of the Promised Land as defined by God—but they will.*

In addition to choosing a people as His own, God also selected a tract of physical land as holy and set apart for Himself. To this very day, the issue of who controls the Promised Land is among the most volatile in international politics. But we need not worry; the right to the Promised Land has already been determined by the only One who has the authority to determine it. The land is called holy because it belongs to God. The Bible tells us that the earth is the Lord's to do with as He wills (Psalm 24:1; Exodus 19:5). In His covenant with Abraham, God designated who would control this land: He gave it to Abraham and his descendants, the people of Israel (Genesis 17:7–8).

Some have suggested that the promise of land to Abraham's descendants should not be taken literally. They say it is merely a symbol that indicates a general blessing, or perhaps the promise of heaven. But the Bible is too specific to let us get by with such ephemeral vagueness. It describes the land in definite terms and outlines it with clear geographical boundaries. Dr. John Walvoord stressed this point when he wrote:

> The term *land* . . . used in the Bible, means exactly what it says. It is not talking about heaven. It is talking about a piece of real estate in the Middle East. After all, if all God was promising Abraham was heaven, he could have stayed in Ur of the Chaldees. Why go on the long journey? Why be a pilgrim and a wanderer? No, God meant land.[1]

The land promised to Abraham takes in much more area than what the present nation of Israel occupies. Genesis 15:18 tells us it stretches all the way from the Mediterranean Sea on the west to the Euphrates River on the east. Ezekiel fixes the northern boundary of Palestine at Hamath, one hundred miles north of Damascus (Ezekiel 48:1), and the southern boundary at Kadesh, about one hundred miles south of Jerusalem (Ezekiel 48:28).

If Israel were currently occupying all the land promised to her, she would control all the holdings of present-day Israel, Lebanon, the West Bank of Jordan, and substantial portions of Syria, Iraq, and Saudi Arabia.

Will the Jews ever realize the fulfillment of the covenant to possess that particular tract of land with clear geographic boundaries promised as an everlasting possession? The prophet Isaiah asserted that it will happen during the Millennium. He prophesied that the Lord would "set His hand again the second time to recover the remnant of His people who are left" (Isaiah 11:11).

REMEMBER: When God speaks with clarity and certainty in His Word, we should trust and believe in His promises and eagerly anticipate their realization in our lives.

GOD'S GUARANTEED PROTECTION

Prophetic Connection: *"I say then, has God cast away His people? Certainly not! For I also am an Israelite, of the seed of Abraham, of the tribe of Benjamin. God has not cast away His people whom He foreknew"* (Romans 11:1–2).

God chose the Jewish people as His own and promised to bless them. Has that promise been fulfilled? Centuries before the Roman emperor Titus destroyed Jerusalem in A.D. 70, Jews had been scattered throughout the world by the Assyrians and Babylonians.

After the fall of Jerusalem to the Romans, this dispersion intensified, and Jews were scattered like chaff in the wind to the four corners of the earth. To appreciate the broad scope and magnitude of Jewish dispersion and persecution, consider the following historical facts:

Before and during World War II, Jews throughout Europe were the target of merciless state-sponsored persecution. In 1933, nine million Jews lived in twenty-one European countries. By 1945, two out of three European Jews had been murdered.[1]

Yet the Jewish people were not snuffed out entirely. As always, a remnant remained:

> Thus says the Lord,
> Who gives the sun for a light by day,
> The ordinances of the moon and the stars for
>   a light by night,
> Who disturbs the sea,
> And its waves roar
> (The Lord of hosts is His name):
>
> "If those ordinances depart
> From before Me, says the Lord,
> Then the seed of Israel shall also cease
> From being a nation before Me forever."
>   (Jeremiah 31:35–36)

As we saw earlier, never has a decimated ancient people managed to retain their individual identity through almost twenty centuries and reestablish their nation in their original homeland. The event was specifically prophesied, and it happened exactly as foretold. It was clearly a miraculous act of God.

Yes, God chose the Jews. He singled them out to be the recipients of His great and unique covenant blessings. But the greater the blessing, the greater the burden they bore for failing God. So, the question is, was it worth it?

It may seem that the sufferings of the Jewish people

outstrip their blessings, but that's because the fullness of their inheritance is yet to come. It is awaiting its hour. In other words, if you think the Jews have not yet been sufficiently blessed, just wait; you haven't seen anything yet. God's promise in its fullness is yet to be kept.

REMEMBER: Despite the evil that appears to be multiplying all around us, God's purposes will stand. He is the Rock when all other ground is shifting sand.

REVIVAL IN ISRAEL

Prophetic Connection: *God has declared that the Jewish people will return to Him not just geographically, but also spiritually.*

I am often asked if Israel's presence in her own land today is the final fulfillment of God's promise to regather His people. Many assume it is, but I have to tell them the answer is no! What is happening in Israel today is primarily the result of a secular Zionist movement, whereas Ezekiel wrote about a spiritual return of God's people to Him when he said:

> I will take you from among the nations, gather you out of all countries, and bring you into your own land. Then I will sprinkle clean water on you, and you shall be clean; I will cleanse you from all your filthiness and from all your idols. I will give you a new heart and put a new spirit within you; I will take the heart of stone out of your flesh and give you a heart of flesh. I will put My Spirit within you and cause you to walk in My statutes, and you will keep My judgments and do them. Then you shall dwell in the land that I gave to your fathers; you shall be My people, and I will be your God. (Ezekiel 36:24–28)

The return of Jews to the refounded nation of Israel is the first stage of that prophesied regathering, but it certainly does not fulfill the requirements of a spiritual return to the Lord.

From the moment of God's promise to Abraham to this present hour, the prophecies concerning Israel's total possession and blessing in the land remain unfulfilled. The most dramatic events lie ahead of us. Israel today is an island of a few million immigrants surrounded by a sea of three hundred million enemies, many of them militant and eager to wipe the tiny nation off the map. From a purely human point of view, it would seem inevitable that, sooner or later, Israel will be destroyed.

The Jewish people have survived by remaining vigilant, but they long for peace. According to the Bible, a future leader will fulfill this longing by brokering a seven-year peace deal with Israel's enemies. But Scripture also tells us that this peace plan will be broken, and Israel will be attacked once again, this time as never before. Countless armies will amass against the boxed-in nation, leaving it with no human hope of victory.

Only Christ's return, His judgment, and His reign will finally bring true peace to Israel. It is then that God's covenant with Abraham will reach its ultimate fulfillment. The Jews will return to the Lord. They will be His people, and He will be their God.

REMEMBER: Though Israel has been chosen by God to be His special people, salvation is found in no one but Jesus Christ. It will only be when the people of Israel turn to Jesus that they will be saved.

AN UNLIKELY ALLIANCE

Prophetic Connection: *Scripture foretells a season when Russia and Iran will join forces against Israel. That alliance has been founded and is growing stronger.*

The prophet Ezekiel foretold a time when Russia would attack Israel. In detailing how the military aggression would take place, the prophet listed a coalition of some of the nations that would join with Russia in the attack.

> "I will turn you around, put hooks into your jaws, and lead you out, with all your army, horses, and horsemen, all splendidly clothed, a great company with bucklers and shields, all of them handling swords. Persia, Ethiopia, and Libya are with them, all of them with shield and helmet." (Ezekiel 38:4–5)

Until March 21, 1935, Persia was the official name of the country we now call Iran. For most of history, though, an alliance between Russia and Persia/Iran seemed highly unlikely. In fact, not once in the past 2,500 years has Russia formed a military connection with Persia/Iran—that is, until now.[1] Today, these two nations have formed a strategic military alliance that continues to be strengthened by the political situation in our world.

Several years ago, in a deal worth more than a billion dollars, Russia agreed to sell missiles and other weaponry to Iran. And the connection is even broader, as Joel C. Rosenberg, former aid to Israeli Prime Minister Benjamin Netanyahu, points out: "Over 1,000 Iranian nuclear scientists have been trained in Russia by senior Russian scientists."[2]

Here is an end-time alliance that was prophesied twenty-five hundred years ago, and in the last few decades it has become a reality. Obviously, the stage is being set for the scenario God described through the prophet Ezekiel. Even though the names of places and people groups have changed, the future battles described in Scripture are certain to come to pass. The God who knows the future also holds it in His hands.

REMEMBER: When it comes to the end times, the Bible is more accurate than the news headlines.

DANIEL'S INCREDIBLE VISION

Prophetic Connection: *A vision recorded in the book of Daniel accurately predicted the rise and fall of empires over the course of centuries. God alone was the source of that vision.*

I've heard some people wonder out loud, "Is there anything in the Bible that offers proof about prophecy? Can we look back at the pages of God's Word and see prophecies not just predicted, but also fulfilled?" The answer, of course, is a resounding yes! And one of the best examples of fulfilled prophecy occurs in the book of Daniel.

More than 2,500 years ago, God gave His servant Daniel a vision of the future that we recognize as the most comprehensive prophetic insight ever given to man. While it was not uncommon for God to communicate to His own people through dreams and visions, it is astounding to realize that He gave this greatest vision of all time not only to Daniel but also to a Babylonian king named Nebuchadnezzar, one of history's most wicked Gentile rulers.

Although the king was secure on his throne with all of his enemies subdued or in captivity, he nevertheless found himself in great anxiety about the future. His anxiety stemmed from a recurring dream sent to him by Almighty God—a vivid, nightmarish dream, and one he could not understand, though he sensed ominous implications within it.

Daniel soon found himself standing before Nebuchadnezzar, who asked him if he could reveal the meaning of his dream. Daniel responded, "There is a God in heaven who reveals secrets, and He has made known to King Nebuchadnezzar what will be in the latter days. Your dream, and the visions of your head upon your bed were these" (Daniel 2:28).

Just as God had sent the dream to Nebuchadnezzar, God had also revealed the dream and its interpretation to Daniel (v. 19). Then came the scene in Nebuchadnezzar's "oval office," as the Jewish prophet stood before the king and unfolded for him the future of his nation. (See Daniel 2:31–45 for Daniel's description and explanation of Nebuchadnezzar's dream.)

The overarching purpose of this vision was to teach Nebuchadnezzar, Daniel, and everyone else on the planet what happens when man puts himself in control. This vision gives us the history of human civilization, written by God Himself. While the events Daniel described that day may seem to come about by the power of kings and armies, he understood that the collapse and rise of empires is all God's doing: "*He* changes the times and the seasons; *He* removes kings and raises up kings; *He* gives wisdom to the wise and knowledge to those who have understanding" (2:21, emphasis added).

REMEMBER: "There is no authority except from God, and the authorities that exist are appointed by God" (Romans 13:1).

THE HISTORY OF THE
WORLD IN A DREAM

Prophetic Connection: *Daniel's vision accurately predicted the rise and fall of several empires, including Babylon, Medo-Persia, Greece, and Rome.*

Through Daniel, God gave King Nebuchadnezzar a composite history of the remaining days of the world. In a dream, the king saw a great statue with a head of gold, chest and arms of silver, belly and thighs of bronze, legs of iron, and feet partly of iron and partly clay.

The first world empire, represented by the statue's head of gold, was Nebuchadnezzar's own kingdom of Babylon (Daniel 2:37–38). Nebuchadnezzar would not have doubted that the head of gold referred to his kingdom since the chief deity of Babylon was Marduk, known as "the god of gold." The historian Herodotus described the image of Marduk as a dazzling sight—a golden statue seated upon a golden throne before a golden table and a golden altar. Pliny tells us the robes of Marduk's priests were interlaced with gold.[1]

The second world empire revealed in the king's dream is represented by the image's chest of silver, from which two silver arms emerge (2:32). When Daniel reported the events surrounding the end of the Babylonian Empire, he stated clearly that it would be the dual monarchy of the Medes and the Persians that would take control of Nebuchadnezzar's empire (5:28).

The third world empire revealed within the image is represented by its belly and thighs of bronze. Daniel told the king it would be a "kingdom of bronze, which shall rule over all the earth" (2:39). Not only does history confirm Greece as the empire that succeeded the Medo-Persians, but Daniel himself affirmed it by naming Greece specifically in Daniel 8:21.

The fourth empire displayed in the image is symbolized by its legs of iron (2:40). History shows us clearly that Rome is the fourth kingdom. Historians often use *iron* as an adjective when characterizing the Roman Empire: Rome's iron grip; Rome's iron rule; Rome's iron legions.

Daniel prophesied that the Roman Empire would be on the earth when God sets up His earthly kingdom. "And in the days of these kings, the God of heaven will set up a kingdom which shall never be destroyed; and the kingdom shall not be left to other people; it shall break in pieces and consume all these kingdoms, and it shall stand forever" (Daniel 2:44).

REMEMBER: There is coming a day when the kingdoms of this world will become the kingdom of our Lord (see Revelation 11:15).

THERE WILL BE A RESURRECTED ROME

Prophetic Connection: *Daniel's own vision points to a reborn Roman Empire that has yet to appear on the world stage.*

Years after Nebuchadnezzar's prophetic dream and Daniel's corresponding vision, Daniel had his own dream, which provided more detail about the nature of the kingdoms he saw. Much of what was revealed to Daniel in these dreams has already happened. But not all of it. Three prophesied kingdoms have come and gone, and the fourth kingdom has also made its appearance in history. But Daniel's later vision included additional information about the future of the fourth kingdom not given to the Babylonian monarch—information about events that are yet in the future.

Let's look at how Daniel describes it:

"After this I saw in the night visions, and behold, a fourth beast, dreadful and terrible, exceedingly strong. It had huge iron teeth; it was devouring, breaking in pieces, and trampling the residue with its feet. It was different from all the beasts that were before it, and it had ten horns." (Daniel 7:7)

Daniel is careful to explain that the ten horns are ten kings who shall arise from this kingdom (v. 24). We know that this ten-kingdom prophecy of Daniel's remains in the future because not only has the ten-leader form of the Roman Empire never existed in history, but neither has such a kingdom been suddenly crushed as prophecy indicates it will be. According to Daniel 2, the Roman Empire in its final form will experience sudden destruction.

The Roman Empire of Jesus' day did not end suddenly. It gradually deteriorated and declined over many centuries until the western part fell in A.D. 476, and the eastern part, the Byzantine Empire, fell in A.D. 1453. You can hardly imagine a more gradual slide from glory to oblivion! We must conclude, then, that some form of the Roman Empire will emerge in the end times and, according to Daniel, it will be in place prior to the coming of Christ to rule and reign over the earth.

The future manifestation of the Roman Empire that Daniel prophesied twenty-five hundred years ago will take the form of a coalition or confederation of ten world leaders and will encompass the same territory as the historic Roman Empire. Today, as we see entities like the European Union, we can see a coalition similar to Daniel's description taking shape right before our eyes!

REMEMBER: The geopolitical landscape of our world will continue to bend and change, but it cannot break free of its prophetic destiny. Everything will come to pass just as God told Daniel.

DANIEL'S PROMISE OF THE ANTICHRIST

Prophetic Connection: *The prophet's vision of the restored Roman Empire lays the groundwork for our understanding of the Antichrist who is still to come.*

According to the prophecy recorded in Daniel 7, a supreme leader will rise from among the ten-leader confederacy in Europe:

> "And another shall rise after them; he shall be different from the first ones, and shall subdue three kings. He shall speak pompous words against the Most High, shall perse- cute the saints of the Most High, and shall intend to change times and law. Then the saints shall be given into his hand for a time and times and half a time." (vv. 24–25)

This leader will emerge from the group of ten to take control of the new European Union. He will become the final world dictator. We know him as the Antichrist. But the point we must not miss now is this: the European Union is one of the conditional preludes to the coming of the Antichrist. As

Arno Froese, executive director of Midnight Call Ministries, wrote:

> The new European power structure will fulfill the prophetic predictions which tell us that a one world system will be implemented. When established, it will fall into the hands of the Antichrist.[1]

We can have little doubt that such a thing could easily happen when we see how glibly statesmen and politicians can gravitate to power. Paul-Henri Spaak, the first president of the UN General Assembly, first president of the European Parliament, and onetime secretary general of NATO, is credited with making this stunning statement:

> We do not need another committee. We have too many already. What we want is a man of sufficient stature to hold the allegiance of all people, and to lift us out of the economic morass into which we are sinking. Send us such a man and be he god or devil, we will receive him.[2]

Statements such as this should chill us to the bone. It shows that the world as a whole in its ignorance will actually embrace the power that will seek to enslave it. The European Union is the kindling awaiting the spark of the Antichrist to inflame the world with unprecedented evil. It is certainly a time to be vigilant.

REMEMBER: "Little children, it is the last hour; and as you have heard that the Antichrist is coming, even now many antichrists have come, by which we know that it is the last hour" (1 John 2:18).

THE THREAT OF
RADICAL ISLAM

Prophetic Connection: *The Bible offers helpful insights for understanding the role of Islam in history and in our current world.*

In 2005, then-president of Iran Mahmoud Ahmadinejad was called before the United Nations Security Council to explain his continued determination to develop nuclear weapons. He began his speech by declaring, "In the Name of the God of Mercy, Compassion, Peace, Freedom and Justice . . ." and ended his speech with this prayer: "I pray to you to hasten the emergence of your last repository, the promised one, that perfect and pure human being, the one that will fill this world with justice and peace."[1]

The "promised one" in Ahmadinejad's prayer was a reference to the Twelfth Imam, a figure in Shi'ite teaching that parallels the figure of Al-Mahdi in Sunni teaching. In essence, both of these titles refer to the Islamic messiah who is yet to come.

Shi'a Islam believes that the Twelfth Imam can appear only during a time of worldwide chaos. This explains why Iran's leadership continues to press forward with their nuclear program in spite of world censure and why they are adamant about destroying Israel.

Decades before the rest of the world began to take Iran's threats seriously, the people of Israel were already totally convinced. They have long understood that militant Islam is determined to destroy them. And the prophet Ezekiel backs up that understanding. He told us that the hatred Persia (now called Iran) bears toward the Jewish nation will play an important role in a major end-times battle. John Walvoord summarizes the scenario:

> The rise of Islamic terror is setting the stage for the events in Ezekiel 38–39. These chapters prophesy an invasion of Israel in the end times by a vast coalition of nations, all of whom are Islamic today except Russia. Israel has said that a new "axis of terror"—Iran, Syria, and the Hamas-run Palestinian government—is sowing the seeds of the first world war of the twenty-first century. The rise of Islam, and especially radical Islamic terrorism, strikingly foreshadows Ezekiel's great prophecy.[2]

Even though the hope for an Islamic messiah is futile, the chaos radical Islamic leaders are creating to bring about that hope is all too real—and deadly. So deadly that much of the biblical prophecies concerning the end times will be brought about by the beliefs and actions of radical Islam. We are beginning to feel the pressure of those impending events in the rise and rapid spread of Islamic radicalism in our own time.

REMEMBER: While radical Islam promises to bring chaos to this world, Jesus is the Prince of Peace; in the end His peace will prevail.

THE WAY, THE TRUTH, AND THE LIFE

Prophetic Connection: *As we study nations and religious systems that will be part of the end times, we must not lose track of the individuals within those systems who need salvation.*

God is at work in the Islamic world. Over the past few decades, we have received reports that many Muslims are being confronted with the gospel in their dreams. Here is the testimony of one Saudi Arabian who grew up going to the mosque five times a day. For many nights, he had a nightmare in which he was being taken down into hell. This dream, always vivid and horrifying, destroyed the man's peace night after night. Suddenly one evening, Jesus appeared in his dream and said, "Son, I am the way, the truth, and the life. And if you would give your life to Me, I would save you from the hell that you have seen."

This young man knew something of Jesus from the distorted teachings of the Qu'ran, but he didn't know the Jesus of the New Testament. So, he began searching for a Christian who could help him. Since Christianity is banned in Saudi Arabia and a Christian caught witnessing to a Muslim could be beheaded, the young man's search took time. But the Lord eventually led him to an Egyptian Christian who gave him a Bible. He began reading, and when he got into the New Testament, he was moved to give his life totally to Jesus Christ.

Soon afterward, the young man's conversion was discovered, and the authorities arrested him. In jail, he was tortured and eventually sentenced to death by beheading. But on the morning of his scheduled execution, no one showed up to escort him from the cell. Two days later the authorities threw open his cell door and screamed at him: "You demon! Get out of this place!"[1]

The man learned later that his execution had not taken place because, on the very day he was to be beheaded, the son of his accuser had mysteriously died. The new Christian is now quietly working to bring other Muslims to faith in Christ.

The rising threat of radical Islam is real and should be taken very seriously. But there is a Christian response to this threat. As someone once said, "The best way to destroy an enemy is to make him a friend." Our prayers, our testimonies, our love and care for our Islamic neighbors may not turn the inevitable tide for the world, but they can turn the tide for individuals and allow them to escape the wrath to come. And that is definitely worth doing.

REMEMBER: "For this is good and acceptable in the sight of God our Savior, who desires all men to be saved and to come to the knowledge of the truth" (1 Timothy 2:3–4).

CAUGHT UP TOGETHER IN THE CLOUDS

Prophetic Connection: *Jesus promised to gather Christians to Himself before the dreadful events of the Tribulation. This moment of gathering is often called the Rapture.*

According to my online dictionary, the word *rapture* means "an expression or manifestation of ecstasy or passion" and "being carried away by overwhelming emotion."[1] But the Bible tells us it means that millions of people will disappear from the face of the earth in less than a millisecond. And that the purpose of that evacuation is to avoid horrific devastation. This evacuation will remove God's people from the disastrous effects of coming earthquakes, fire, and global chaos.

Rapture is the Latin version of a phrase the Bible uses to describe the catching away of all Christians before the end times. The Lord will descend with a shout and a trumpet of God. All believers, living and dead, will suddenly meet the Lord in the air.

When the Bible speaks of the Rapture, the focus is not from the viewpoint of those who remain on earth, but from those who are evacuated. Before the seven-year Tribulation breaks out, all true followers of the Lord will be caught up from the earth and delivered right into the presence of the Lord. The Rapture will fulfill the promise Jesus made to His disciples in John 14:1–3:

> "Let not your heart be troubled; you believe in God, believe also in Me. In My Father's house are many mansions; if it were not so, I would have told you. I go to prepare a place for you. And if I go and prepare a place for you, I will come again and receive you to Myself; that where I am, there you may be also."

Followers of Christ who are raptured will be spared the trauma of death and the coming disasters that will occur when the Tribulation breaks out upon the earth. That is indeed a cause for true rapture on the part of those who love the Lord and long to be with Him.

The New Testament indicates that the rapture of those who have put their trust in Christ is the next major event on the prophetic calendar. In other words, the Rapture awaits us on the horizon—it could happen at any moment.

REMEMBER: "Then we who are alive and remain shall be caught up together with them in the clouds to meet the Lord in the air. And thus we shall always be with the Lord" (1 Thessalonians 4:17).

A TALE OF TWO RETURNS

Prophetic Connection: *The Rapture and the Second Coming are two separate events on God's prophetic calendar.*

When I preach on the events of the end times, some people mistakenly think I contradict myself. You see, I speak about prophecies that must be fulfilled prior to Christ's Second Coming, but then I am also sure to say nothing needs to happen before Jesus returns to claim His own; it can happen at any moment. This honest and all-too-common confusion deserves to be addressed because I believe many people are puzzled.

Most of the misunderstanding comes from confusing two separate events: the Rapture and the Second Coming. When we talk about the signs that signal the return of Christ, we speak not of the Rapture but of the Lord's ultimate return to the earth with all His saints. While the Rapture will be a "stealth event" in which Christ will be witnessed by believers only, His second coming, seven years later, will be a public event. Everyone will see Him.

All believers will be raptured. He will immediately take them back into heaven with Him. But when Christ returns to earth seven years later at the Second Coming, He is coming to stay. This return will take place at the end of the Tribulation period and usher in the Millennium—a thousand-year reign of Christ on this earth.

So, the Rapture will occur seven years before the Second Coming. At that time Christ will take us to be with Him in heaven, immediately before the seven-year Tribulation period. Then, we will return to earth with Him at His Second Coming.

There are no events that must take place between now and the Rapture. It's all a matter of God's perfect timing. When I preach that signs are developing concerning the Lord's return, I am referring to events that must yet occur before the return of Christ in the Second Coming.

The prophecies I speak of concern the Second Coming, but that does not mean that the Rapture doesn't figure into prophecy. Since the Rapture takes place seven years before the Second Coming, the signs that point to the Second Coming cast shadows that clue us in to the imminent Rapture. The fact that the Rapture precedes the Second Coming makes the signs portending Jesus' public return all the more immediate and ominous. For those who are left behind, the Rapture will give irrefutable confirmation of end-time events, seven years before they come to pass.

REMEMBER: "Behold, He is coming with clouds, and every eye will see Him, even they who pierced Him. And all the tribes of the earth will mourn because of Him. Even so, Amen" (Revelation 1:7).

SAY NO TO SORROW

Prophetic Connection: *The promise of the Rapture as a future event should provide hope for all believers—even as we deal with the reality of death.*

First Thessalonians 4:13–18 tells us all we need to know about the Rapture. Let's look more deeply into what Paul said. First, he wrote: "But I do not want you to be ignorant, brethren, concerning those who have fallen asleep, lest you sorrow as others who have no hope" (1 Thessalonians 4:13). In this statement, the apostle addressed the ignorance of the Thessalonians concerning the state of those who had died believing in Christ. The word he used to describe that state has great significance for every believer today. Paul said they had "fallen asleep." For the word translated *asleep*, he used the Greek word *koimao*, which has as one of its meanings, "to sleep in death." The same word is used to describe the deaths of Lazarus, Stephen, David, and Jesus Christ (John 11:11; Acts 7:60; 13:36; and 1 Corinthians 15:20).

In the next part of the Thessalonian passage, we find Paul affirming the Thessalonians' hopes that their loved ones will live again. He did this by tying that hope to the Resurrection and the Rapture: "Lest you sorrow as others who have no hope. For if we believe that Jesus died and rose again, even so God will bring with Him those who sleep in Jesus" (1 Thessalonians 4:13–14). Here Paul tells the Thessalonians (and us) that God's plan for our future gives us such a new perspective on death that when someone we love dies, we need not be overcome with sorrow and despair, for on that day when those who are alive in Christ are raptured, those who died in Christ will be raised to be with Him as well.

Paul reasoned that Christians can believe this promise of resurrection because it is backed up by the resurrection of Christ Himself. The logic is simple: if we believe that Jesus died and rose again, is it hard to believe His promise that He can perform the same miracle for us and those we love?

REMEMBER: "Neither death nor life, nor angels nor principalities nor powers, nor things present nor things to come, nor height nor depth, nor any other created thing, shall be able to separate us from the love of God which is in Christ Jesus our Lord" (Romans 8:38–39).

COME FORTH!

Prophetic Connection: *The Rapture will not be a generic event; it will be a rescue mission through which Christ will seek out individuals and raises them heavenward.*

Paul states in 1 Thessalonians, "For the Lord Himself will descend from heaven with a shout, with the voice of an archangel, and with the trumpet of God" (4:16). As you read these words, the Lord Jesus Christ is seated in the heavens at the right hand of the Father. But when the right moment comes, Jesus will initiate the Rapture by literally and physically rising from the throne, stepping into the corridors of light, and actually descending into the atmosphere of planet Earth, from which He rose into the heavens over the Mount of Olives two thousand years ago. It is not the angels or the Holy Spirit, but the Lord Himself who is coming to draw believers into the heavens at the Rapture.

The details of this passage paint an amazingly complete sensory picture of the Rapture. Paul even gave the sounds that will be heard—a shout, the voice of an archangel, and the trumpet of God. The purpose and relationship of these three sounds have generated considerable discussion. Some claim the shout is for the church, the archangel's voice is for the Jews, and the trumpet is for all Gentile believers. But these claims are mistaken. The three allusions to sounds are not to be taken as separate but rather as singular. Paul was not describing three separate sounds; he was describing only one sound in three different ways.

This sound will be like a shout, ringing with authority like the voice of an archangel. It will also be like the blare of a trumpet in its volume and clarity. And the sound will be exclusively directed—heard only by those who have placed their trust in Christ. When Jesus raised Lazarus from the dead, he shouted, "Lazarus, come forth!" (John 11:43). I've heard Bible students speculate as to what might have happened had Jesus forgotten to mention Lazarus's name. Would all the dead within the range of His voice have emerged from their graves? At the Rapture, that is exactly what will happen. His shout of "Come forth!" will not name a single individual, but it will be heard by every believer in every grave around the world. All those tombs will empty, and the resurrected believers will fly skyward.

REMEMBER: The promise of the Rapture is for all who have trusted Jesus as their Lord and Savior. If you are in Christ, you will be called heavenward!

NO MORE SALT AND LIGHT

Prophetic Connection: *The Rapture will trigger the events of the Tribulation in part because all believers will be removed from the world, leaving only darkness behind.*

Today as never before, we are beginning to see the signs of our Lord's impending return. But it is the Rapture that will trigger the cataclysmic upheavals that will ravage the earth for the seven years that follow it. The Tribulation will come about by the law of natural consequences.

According to Jesus, Christians are the salt and light of the world (Matthew 5:13–14). Salt prevents decay; light proclaims truth. When all the Christians in the entire world are removed from the earth in one day, all the salt and all the light will suddenly be gone. The result is predictable. You may think the world today is degenerating into rampant greed and immorality, and indeed it is. But as bad as things are becoming, we can hardly overstate the horror that will occur when society loses the tempering influence of Christians.

As the Bible teaches, every believer in Christ is indwelt by the Holy Spirit. This means the Holy Spirit ministers to today's world through followers of Christ. When all Christians are removed from the earth, the restraining ministry of the

Holy Spirit will be completely absent. The result will be horrific. Jesus Himself described what will happen next: "For then there will be great tribulation, such as has not been since the beginning of the world until this time, no, nor ever shall be. And unless those days were shortened, no flesh would be saved" (Matthew 24:21–22).

As these dire words are being fulfilled during the Tribulation period, we who are followers of Christ will have already been raptured to heaven. This is a source of great comfort for Christians. No promise has been more precious to believers than the one made to the church of Philadelphia in Revelation: "Because you have kept My command to persevere, I also will keep you from the hour of trial which shall come upon the whole world, to test those who dwell on the earth" (Revelation 3:10).

Please note that our Lord's promise is not merely to keep us *in* the hour of trial, but rather *from* the hour of trial. As Paul wrote, "God did not appoint us to wrath, but to obtain salvation through our Lord Jesus Christ" (1 Thessalonians 5:9). The promise is that we who are believers will not experience the horrors of the Tribulation, and this is an enormous source of comfort.

REMEMBER: Just as the church's absence will bring great chaos and suffering to the world during the Tribulation, the presence of believers in the world today is a tremendous blessing to all people.

A TIME OF TROUBLE

Prophetic Connection: *Jesus warned us about the conditions of the world prior to the Rapture and the Tribulation.*

Recorded in Matthew 24, the Olivet Discourse may have been Jesus' final sermon. In it, He described what the conditions of the world will be like prior to the Rapture, the Tribulation, and the Second Coming. Those days will be filled with "signs" that Jesus said will occur like "birth pains." Meaning, those signs will occur with greater frequency and greater intensity until Christ steps out of heaven to reclaim His own.

Jesus' words reveal ten signs or events we can expect to experience in embryonic form during the days preceding the Rapture and the beginning of the Tribulation. Even after the Rapture, these ten signs will continue to multiply and progress as the first three and one-half years of the Great Tribulation unfold.

- A Time of Deception—"Many will come in My name, saying, 'I am the Christ,' and will deceive many" (Matthew 24:5).

- A Time of Dissension—"You will hear of wars and rumors of wars. . . . Nation will rise against nation, and kingdom against kingdom" (24:6–7).
- A Time of Devastation—"There will be famines" (24:7).
- A Time of Disease—" . . . pestilences . . ." (24:7).
- A Time of Disasters—" . . . and earthquakes in various places" (24:7).
- A Time of Death—"They will deliver you up to tribulation and kill you, and you will be hated by all nations for My name's sake" (24:9).
- A Time of Disloyalty—"Many will be offended, will betray one another, and will hate one another" (24:10).
- A Time of Delusion—"Many false prophets will rise up and deceive many" (24:11). It should also be noted that part of the delusion will be an increase in drug use. One of the characteristics of the end times' false religion will be what the book of Revelation calls "sorceries" (9:21). The word John uses is *pharmakia*, from which we get the word *pharmacy*. It is an ancient reference to the ingestion of drugs. The use of mind-altering substances such as narcotics and hallucinogens will be associated with false religions, doubtless with the approval of the government.
- A Time of Defection—"Because lawlessness will abound, the love of many will grow cold" (Matthew 24:12). People will turn away from God and from one another.

- A Time of Declaration—"This gospel of the kingdom will be preached in all the world as a witness to all the nations" (24:14).

REMEMBER: For the believer, the signs of the Lord's soon coming are a source of joy, not dread. Though the world may be growing darker, in the end His light will shine all the brighter!

BE READY FOR WHAT'S COMING

Prophetic Connection: *Scripture affirms that Christ may initiate the Rapture at any moment; therefore, all people should make themselves ready for that inevitable day.*

There's a danger in thinking about prophetic events as merely "historical" rather than "personal." Without a doubt, the Rapture and the Tribulation will become personal for all who experience them!

Therefore, as we look forward to the day the Lord will return for His followers, Scripture calls us to stay ready by living pure and holy lives:

> For the grace of God that brings salvation has appeared to all men, teaching us that, denying ungodliness and worldly lusts, we should live soberly, righteously, and godly in the present age, looking for the blessed hope and glorious appearing of our great God and Savior Jesus Christ, who gave Himself for us, that He might redeem us from every lawless deed and purify for Himself His own special people, zealous for good works. (Titus 2:11–14)

We are admonished to live as if Jesus could come at any moment. The fact is, He can.

God has sounded the warnings loudly and clearly. They have come through His prophets in the Old Testament, through New Testament writers, and even through Jesus Himself. The firestorm is coming in the form of the seven years of tribulation, when no Christian influence will temper the evil that will plunge the earth into a cauldron of misery and devastation. But you can avoid that destruction and be evacuated. You can enter your name on the list of those who will hear the trumpet call of the Rapture by turning to Christ and beginning to live the pure and holy life that characterizes those who will enter heaven. As the apostle John wrote: "But there shall by no means enter it [the heavenly city of God] anything that defiles, or causes an abomination or a lie, but only those who are written in the Lamb's Book of Life" (Revelation 21:27).

If your name is not in that book when the Rapture occurs, you will be left behind to experience horrors worse than anything the world has yet seen. I hope you will not wait another day; turn to Jesus Christ now, before it is too late, and become one of those who will hear His call on that great and terrible day.

REMEMBER: "Therefore you also be ready, for the Son of Man is coming at an hour you do not expect" (Matthew 24:44).

GOD BLESS AMERICA

Prophetic Connection: *The United States does not seem to be directly mentioned in the prophetic passages of Scripture, yet God is using America to accomplish His will.*

Every day when the sun rises over Washington, D.C., its first rays fall on the eastern side of the city's tallest structure, the 555-foot-high Washington Monument, where these words are inscribed: *Laus Deo*, Latin for "Praise be to God." This compact prayer of praise, visible to the eyes of heaven alone, is tacit recognition of our nation's unique acknowledgment of the place of God in its founding and its continuance.[1]

Were these words merely a grandiose but empty claim to national piety, or do they reflect a true reality? President Ronald Reagan believed that God has a plan for our nation. He wrote, "I have always believed that this anointed land was set apart in an uncommon way, that a divine plan placed this great continent here between the oceans to be found by people from every corner of the earth who had a special love of faith and freedom."[2]

It seems clear to me that God does have a plan for America. It is true that we have no direct reference to that plan in the Old or New Testaments, but that does not discount the evident fact that God has a sovereign purpose for America in His redemptive plan.

Why has America, in her short history, outstripped the wealth, power, and influence of all ancient and modern civilizations? Can God have blessed a nation so richly without reserving for her a pivotal purpose? Clearly America did not become the land of the free and the home of the brave by blind fate or a happy set of coincidences. Our leaders, throughout our history, have understood this. That is why, through season after season, they have turned to God for guidance. We see Washington kneeling in the snow of Valley Forge. We see our Founding Fathers on their knees at the first Continental Congress. We see the gaunt Lincoln praying in the hour of national crisis.

George Washington summarized this national dependence on God, which was evident before his time and continued after him, when he said, "No people can be bound to acknowledge and adore the invisible hand which conducts the affairs of man more than those of the United States."[3]

REMEMBER: Although America is not specifically mentioned in Scripture, God's special care for this nation has been evident throughout its storied history.

TO THE ENDS OF THE EARTH

Prophetic Connection: *Scripture promises that everyone in the world will have a chance to hear the gospel before the end. America has been instrumental in the fulfillment of that promise.*

What role will American play in the end times? The answer is uncertain. But there's no doubt about the role America *has played* and *is playing* to advance the coming of God's kingdom: "To the United States belongs the distinction of providing three-fourths of the missionaries of the last century and approximately the same amount of money and material aid."[1] This means that 75 percent of all missionaries in the twentieth century came from a country boasting only 5 percent of the total world population. God blesses those who make His priorities their priorities.

God loves the world. He loves the people who have yet to hear the gospel. When we love whom He loves, He blesses us. And I believe that principle applies to our nation as well as to the church.

God has blessed America because we have been the launching pad for the world's great missionary movement. In the aftermath of World War II, Americans started 1,800 missions agencies and sent out more than 350,000 missionaries.[2] As a result, "today, 95 percent of the world's population have access not only to some portion of Scripture in their language but also to Christian radio broadcasts, audio recordings, and the Jesus film."[3] That achievement is due largely to the missionary zeal of churches in the United States.

Is it any wonder, then, that Satan has placed a big, bright target on America and its people? By supporting and sending missionaries throughout the world, U.S. churches are bringing light to the darkness and waging a battle against the demonic forces at work in various places. By leaps and bounds, American missionaries have brought us closer to fulfilling Jesus' words in Matthew 24: "And this gospel of the kingdom will be preached in all the world as a witness to all the nations, and then the end will come" (v. 14). America may not be mentioned in Scripture as having a role to play in end-times events, but there can be little doubt our nation's historic commitment to spreading the gospel has indeed shaped the course of world history.

REMEMBER: Like no other nation in history, the United States has answered the call of Psalm 96:3, which says, "Declare His glory among the nations, His wonders among all peoples."

WILL AMERICA FALL BEFORE THE END?

Prophetic Connection: *Biblical prophecy helps us understand what role American may play during the end times.*

In light of the fact that America, the lone superpower in the world today, is not mentioned in biblical prophecies concerning the end of the age, many believers have asked, "Why not?" There are several possible answers to that question. Perhaps, through treaties, the U.S. will become part of a European coalition—the new Roman Empire. It's also possible, devastating as it might be to imagine, that America will be decimated by war before the end comes. Or perhaps the United States will be so compromised by moral decay that it will no longer play a vital role on the world stage.

But there is another possibility. If the Rapture were to happen today and all the true believers in Jesus Christ disappeared into heaven in a single moment, America as we know it could be obliterated. It is estimated that at the Rapture, America will lose millions of citizens—all its Christians and their small children.[1] Not only would our country lose a significant percentage of her population, but she would also lose the very best, the "salt" and "light" of the nation. Who can imagine the chaos in our country when all the godly people disappear—enough to populate many vast cities—leaving only those who have rejected God? It is not a pretty picture.

In an article about the United States in prophecy, Herman A. Hoyt wrote:

> Since the promise of Christ's coming for the Church has always been held out to His people as an event that could take place at any moment, surely the events of the present hour in relation to the United States ought to give new stimulus to watch momentarily for His coming. In these days of crisis, our trust should not rest in a nation that may shortly disappear, but in Him who works all things after the counsel of His own will.[2]

Amen. Our hope is not found in a nation. Our trust has never been in governments, civilizations, or cultures. By the standards of eternity, these institutions last but a moment, crumbling into dust to be swept away by the winds of history. They are helpful while they are here, but they have never been worthy of our trust. Christians have always put our trust in the One who stands above institutions, above history, and even above time itself—the One by whose power and permission these things exist, and who knows their times and the ends of their days. Only He is worthy of our ultimate allegiance.

REMEMBER: America is not "the last best hope of earth," as Abraham Lincoln famously said. That honor belongs to Jesus Christ alone.

HOW THEN SHALL WE LIVE?

Prophetic Connection: *"Now learn this parable from the fig tree: When its branch has already become tender and puts forth leaves, you know that summer is near. So you also, when you see all these things, know that it is near—at the doors!" (Matthew 24:32–33)*

With America seemingly left out of end-times prophecy, it would be possible to look at the spiritual state of our nation and grow discouraged. But living with the hope of the Rapture encourages Christians to do three things.

Keep on waiting. In Matthew 24:32–34, Jesus used the fig tree as a metaphor for Israel, telling the disciples to watch for it to begin putting forth leaves. In other words, He encouraged them to be cognizant of what was happening around them as they waited for events to unfold.

We can apply that same lesson as we wait for the unfolding of the end times. We are waiting still, but our waiting is growing shorter. We can wait with the confidence that God's purposes are going to be worked out. Jesus said, "But of that day and hour no one knows, not even the angels of heaven, but My Father only" (v. 36).

Keep on working. Our task while we wait for the return of Christ is clear: to continue to labor in the Master's vineyard until His return. Many Christians throughout church history have made the mistake of supposing they knew the time of Christ's return and ceased from their labors. They have retreated from the world only to be disappointed when their expectations proved false. Jesus himself said, "I must work the works of Him who sent Me while it is day; the night is coming when no one can work" (John 9:4). That must be our passion as well—to do the work of Christ while we have the opportunity. When night comes the opportunity will have passed. "Blessed is that servant whom his master, when he comes, will find [serving]" (Matt. 24:46).

Keep watching. Finally, we are to keep watching—looking to the sky, as it were, for His return. In Luke 21:28 we find these words of Jesus: "Now when these things begin to happen, look up and lift up your heads, because your redemption draws near."

Southern evangelist Vance Havner gave us the real key to keeping to our task and finding joy in the face of impending doom: "We are not just looking for something to happen, we are looking for Someone to come! And when these things begin to come to pass, we are not to drop our heads in discouragement, or shake our heads in despair, but we are to lift our heads in delight."[1]

Remember: Watch with joy and expectation for Christ's return!

THE RULER OF THE WORLD

Prophetic Connection: *Scripture shows us that, during the seven years of the Tribulation, the world will come under the control of a hellish dictator called the Antichrist.*

When I first began studying prophecy more than forty years ago, I encountered the Bible's prediction that one man would eventually take control of the entire world. Frankly, I could not imagine how such a thing would ever happen. But since the Bible presented this as a major part of the end-times landscape, I believed it, and I preached it even though I could not comprehend it.

Today it is much easier to envision the possibility of such a world ruler. Technology has given us instant global communication. Twenty-four hour news channels are seen everywhere in the world. The Internet and satellite cell phones reach every country on the face of the earth. Air transportation has shrunk the planet to the point where we can set foot on the soil of any nation in a matter of hours. I am told that there are now missiles that can reach any part of the world in fewer than thirty minutes. People and nations no longer live in isolation.

There are also other factors that make the ascendance

of a global leader more plausible than ever before. The Bible predicts that worldwide chaos, instability, and disorder will increase as we approach the end of this age. Jesus Himself said that there would be wars, rumors of wars, famines, and earthquakes in various places (Matthew 24:6-7). Just before these tensions explode into world chaos, the Rapture of the church will depopulate much of the planet. Millions of people could suddenly disappear from our nation alone.

The devastation wrought by these disasters will spur a worldwide outcry for relief and order at almost any cost. That will set the stage for the emergence of a new world leader who will, like a pied piper, promise a solution to all problems. He will negotiate world peace and promise order and security. This leader, who will emerge out of the newly formed European Union, is commonly referred to in the Bible as the Antichrist.

REMEMBER: "Every spirit that confesses that Jesus Christ has come in the flesh is of God, and every spirit that does not confess that Jesus Christ has come in the flesh is not of God. And this is the spirit of the Antichrist, which you have heard was coming, and is now already in the world" (1 John 4:2-3).

SATAN'S SUPERMAN

Prophetic Connection: *The Antichrist will not be a regular person; he will be directly empowered by the Devil.*

The very word *antichrist* sends a shudder through the hearts of Christians. All have heard or read of him, and the fear that some feel at the mention of his name comes largely from misunderstandings and confusion about who he is, when he will appear, and what powers he can exercise over God's people. So, let's dispel those fears and clear up the confusion.

The word *antichrist* is used four times in the New Testament, each time by the apostle John, and it is found only in his epistles (1 John 2:18, 22; 4:3; 2 John 7). As the word suggests, the Antichrist is a person who is against Christ. The prefix *anti* can also mean "instead of," and both meanings will apply to this coming world leader. He will overtly oppose Christ and at the same time pass himself off as Christ.

The Antichrist will aggressively live up to his terrible name. He will be Satan's superman who persecutes, tortures, and kills the people of God and leads the armies of the world into the climactic Battle of Armageddon. He will be the most powerful dictator the world has ever seen, making Caesar, Hitler, Mao, and Saddam seem weak and tame by comparison.

Even though the Antichrist is identified by that name only four times in the Bible, he appears many more times under various aliases.

He is also called:

- "the prince who is to come" (Daniel 9:26)
- a "fierce" king (8:23)
- a "master of intrigue" (8:23 NIV)
- a "despicable man" (11:21 NLT)
- a "worthless shepherd" (Zechariah 11:16–17 NLT)
- the "one who brings destruction" (2 Thessalonians 2:3 NLT)
- the "lawless one" (2:8)
- the "beast" (Revelation 13:1)

Put together, these names and descriptions paint a chilling picture of this ruler who will oppose Christ and lead the world astray. And yet, we know his reign will end in defeat, for God will have the final victory!

REMEMBER: The Antichrist will be a counterfeit Christ, because Satan can only imitate and corrupt, never innovate or create.

A MAN OF MYSTERY

Prophetic Connection: *God's Word offers a great deal of helpful information about the Antichrist. Yet it does not reveal his identity.*

Though the Bible describes the Antichrist in detail, it never identifies him by name. However, that has not stopped speculation on who he might be and even the out-right naming of certain individuals. Many names have been suggested. When you google "Who is Antichrist?" you get about 12.5 million hits. Some of the Web sites post incredibly long and detailed articles—a sign of the extreme fascination generated by this sensational subject.

I have a pamphlet in my file called *The Beast: The False Prophet and Hitler.* It was published in 1941, the year I was born. This pamphlet presented the formula for identifying Hitler as the Antichrist by showing how the letters in the word Hitler link him numerologically with the "number of the beast" given in Revelation 13:16–18:

> He causes all, both small and great, rich and poor, free and slave, to receive a mark on their right hand or on their foreheads, and that no one may buy or sell except one who

has the mark or the name of the beast, or the number of his name. Here is wisdom. Let him who has understanding calculate the number of the beast, for it is the number of a man: His number is 666.

The pamphlet bases its conclusion on a numerological formula. Some biblical numerologists tell us that the number 666, when worked out through a transposition of number assignments to alphabetical letters, will identify the name of a certain man. In the Revelation passage we have only three numerals—666—but according to numerology, through these numbers we can find the man's name. The first step is to assign numbers to the letters in the alphabet: you let 100 stand for A, 101 for B, 102 for C, and so on through the rest of the letters. Then you take Hitler's name and give each letter its numerical value: H=107, I=108, T=119, L=111, E=104, R=117. Now, add up these six numbers, and voilà! The total is 666! So, obviously Hitler must be the Antichrist.

To get the most fun out of the "Who's the Antichrist?" game, follow three rules: If the proper name doesn't reach the right total, add a title. If the sum can't be found in English, try Hebrew, Greek, or Latin. Don't be too particular about the spelling. And be persistent; keep working at it, and you can make anybody the Antichrist!

REMEMBER: God has not commanded us to figure out the Antichrist's identity. Our task is to be salt and light in the world while we live in anticipation of Jesus' return.

CHARISMA, DECEPTION, EVIL, AND PRIDE

Prophetic Connection: *Scripture reveals several character traits of the future Antichrist—many of which will make him a poignant and powerful leader.*

The prophet Daniel described the Antichrist in these graphic terms: "After this I saw in the night visions, and behold, a fourth beast. . . . And there . . . were eyes like the eyes of a man, and a mouth speaking pompous words. . . . He shall speak pompous words against the Most High" (Daniel 7:7–8, 25).

In this passage, Daniel gives us one of the characteristics of the coming world ruler—his charismatic personality enhanced by his speaking ability, which he will use to sway the masses with spellbinding words of power and promise. We little realize the power of good speaking ability. An actor who is not classically handsome can land great parts and charm audiences simply by the power of his resonant and articulate voice.

Often Americans are swayed by political candidates who have little to offer, but they offer it in a beautiful package of smooth intonation and syntax. As Daniel says, the coming world leader will be renowned for this kind of eloquence, which will capture the attention and admiration of the world.

Daniel goes on to tell us that this golden-tongued orator not only will speak in high-blown terms but also will utter pompous words against God. The apostle John described him in a similar fashion in the book of Revelation: "And he was given a mouth speaking great things and blasphemies" (Revelation 13:5).

Daniel continues his description of the Antichrist by telling us he is a man "whose appearance was greater than his fellows" (Daniel 7:20). In terms of his outward appearance, this man will be a strikingly attractive person. The combination of magnetic personality, speaking ability, and extreme good looks will make him virtually irresistible to the masses. When he comes on the scene, people will flock to him, and they will fall over themselves to do anything he asks.

Though the church will be raptured prior to the unveiling of the Antichrist, there is a lesson for us all in the descriptions we read in Scripture. We should never allow ourselves to be swayed by the allure of someone's appearance or their silver tongue. True discernment always requires a deeper look.

REMEMBER: Satan is the master of deception who disguises himself as an angel of light (2 Corinthians 11:14). Therefore, we must stand our ground against him by "putting on the belt of truth and the body armor of God's righteousness" (Ephesians 6:14).

PEACE IN THE MIDDLE EAST?

Prophetic Connection: *The Antichrist will be a cunning leader; he will establish his credentials by securing a peace treaty between Israel and her enemies.*

In the famous dream recorded in the seventh chapter of his book, Daniel was given a picture of the Antichrist: "I was considering the horns, and there was another horn, a little one, coming up among them, before whom three of the first horns were plucked out by the roots" (7:8). If we read carefully and understand the symbolic meaning of the horns, we learn from this verse that the coming world leader will subdue three other kings by plucking them out by their roots. He will take over three kingdoms one by one, not by making war but by clever political manipulation.

The Antichrist will begin as the little horn, but then he will succeed in uprooting three of the first horns, thus seizing their power for himself. This event is reiterated in the eleventh chapter of Daniel. We read that this future world leader "shall come in peaceably, and seize the kingdom by intrigue" (Daniel 11:21). The Antichrist will be a political genius, a masterful diplomat, and a clever leader.

Arthur W. Pink wrote of him:

> Satan has had full opportunity afforded him to study fallen human nature. . . . The devil knows full well how to dazzle people by the attraction of power. . . . He knows how to gratify the craving for knowledge. . . . He can delight the ear with music and the eye with entrancing beauty. . . . He knows how to exalt people to dizzying heights of worldly greatness and fame, and how to control the greatness so that it may be employed against God and His people.[1]

In today's world, every leader wants to be the one who solves the perpetual crisis in the Middle East. Jimmy Carter thought he had achieved it at Camp David. Bill Clinton tried frantically to eke out a settlement during the final months of his administration. George W. Bush also sought to broker such a peace agreement. Donald Trump made significant progress with the Abraham Accords, and yet today there is still no "road map to world peace." But where all these men failed, the Antichrist will succeed. A cunning leader in love with his own power, he will broker peace and solve the most difficult of geopolitical puzzles. At that point, virtually no one will question his brilliant leadership.

REMEMBER: It is not only the Antichrist who will lead people astray. The Bible warns there will come a time when people "will gather around them a great number of teachers to say what their itching ears want to hear" (2 Timothy 4:3 NIV).

THE WRATH OF A TYRANT

Prophetic Connection: *While the Antichrist will appear peace-loving for a time, Scripture shows that his evil intentions will burst forth in a burning passion to dominate and destroy.*

Once again, we turn to the writings of Daniel to understand the personality of this coming tyrant, the Antichrist:

> Thus he said: "The fourth beast shall be a fourth kingdom on earth, which shall be different from all other kingdoms, and shall devour the whole earth, trample it and break it in pieces. . . . He shall speak pompous words against the Most High, shall persecute the saints of the Most High, and shall intend to change times and law. Then the saints shall be given into his hand for a time and times and half a time." (Daniel 7:23, 25)

The Antichrist is going to devour the whole world. He will break it in pieces. Although all the believers of the present age will be taken to heaven before the reign of this man, new converts will come to Christ during the years of tribulation. This will infuriate the Antichrist, and he will take out his wrath on these new Christians. Many followers of Christ will be martyred for their faith.

The word translated "persecute" in Daniel 7:25 literally means "to wear out." The use of the word here indicates a slow, painful wearing down of the people of God—a torturous, cruel persecution reminiscent of the horrors Nero inflicted on Christians in ancient Rome, but even worse.

We find a prototype of what is to come in the regime of Hitler. Charles Colson offers us a chilling description of what went on in Nazi concentration camps:

> The first Nazi concentration camp opened in 1933. In one camp, hundreds of Jewish prisoners survived in disease-infested barracks on little food and gruesome, backbreaking work. Each day the prisoners were marched to the compound's giant factory, where tons of human waste and garbage were distilled into alcohol to be used as a fuel additive. Even worse than the nauseating smell was the realization that they were fueling the Nazi war machine.[1]

Hitler and the Nazis did not annihilate the Jews all at once; they deliberately and systematically wore down their souls. That gives us a picture of what will happen during the Tribulation when the Antichrist is in power. He will be a cruel, blood-shedding leader, taking out his wrath on the saints who come to Christ under his regime.

REMEMBER: Now is the age of grace, the time of God's favor. The Lord has made a way to escape the wrath of the Antichrist. If you have not done so already, call on God today!

A LION ON A LEASH

Prophetic Connection: *While it may seem like the Antichrist has unlimited power, Scripture reveals that God will remain in control even throughout the Tribulation.*

The four major kingdoms depicted in Daniel's prophetic vision in Daniel 7 were likened to certain animals: Babylon was like a lion, Medo-Persia was like a bear, Greece was like a leopard, and Rome was like the ten-horned beast. In Revelation 13:2, we have all of these characteristics combined into one horrific creature. This likeness of the Antichrist to ferocious beasts is meant to show us the intimidating presence of this satanic creature. He combines in his person all of the threatening characteristics of the kingdoms which have gone before him.

Dr. W.A. Criswell wrote:

Think of the golden majesty of Babylon. Of the mighty ponderous massiveness of Cyrus the Persian. Think of the beauty and the elegance and the intellect of the ancient Greek world. Think of the Roman with his laws and his order and his idea of justice. All of these glories will be summed up in the majesty of this one eventual Antichrist who will be like Nebuchadnezzar, like Cyrus, like Tiglath Pileser, like Shalmaneser, like Julius Caesar, like Caesar Augustus, like Alexander the Great, like Napoleon Bonaparte, like Frederick the Great and Charlemagne, all bound up into one.[1]

As both Daniel and John show us, the Antichrist will be a terrifying person, the epitome of evil, the ultimate negation of everything good, the avowed enemy and despiser of God. At the same time, we must not forget that this satanic creature is not equal to God. He does not have absolute power or anything close to it. God has him on a chain. In fact, in Revelation 13, we are reminded repeatedly that the Antichrist can only do what he is allowed to do.

Twice in this chapter, we find the little phrase, *and he was given.* "And he was given a mouth speaking great things and blasphemies, and he was given authority to continue for forty-two months" (v. 5). We also find in the same chapter, "It was granted to him to make war with the saints and to overcome them. And authority was given him over every tribe, tongue, and nation" (v. 7). As in the story of Job, Satan (and his puppet, the Antichrist) will be able to do only that which God allows. The Antichrist will be able to create terrible havoc and chaos, but ultimately God is still God, and no enemy of His will go beyond the boundaries He sets.

REMEMBER: Even when evil appears to be winning the battle—when life is difficult and hope is hard to find—God is still on His throne.

THE USURPER'S DOWNFALL

Prophetic Connection: *Through a variety of events and demands, the Antichrist will live up to his title by attempting to usurp the role of Jesus in our world.*

One of the first acts of the Antichrist will be to make peace with Israel. And he will keep this covenant during the first three and a half years of his rule. At that point, however, he will change his tactics. He will drop all pretenses of peace and adopt a program of crushing power. He will break his covenant with Israel and subject the Jews to great persecution (Daniel 9:27; Isaiah 28:18). Then will come the leader's most sensational moment: the Antichrist will actually be killed, but to the astonishment of all the world, he will be raised back to life by the power of Satan in a grotesque counterfeit of the resurrection of Jesus Christ (Revelation 13:3–4).

After his death and satanic resurrection, the Antichrist will undermine the leaders of three countries in the European Union, and then all other nations will immediately relinquish their power to him. It is then that he will set himself up to be worshipped by all the people of the world.

Through his associate, the false prophet, the mark of the beast will be placed upon all those who follow him. Anyone who does not bear this mark will be unable to buy or sell in the world's economy. In times past, the idea of a mark that would individually identify everyone in the world for governmental control seemed a far-fetched fantasy, possible only in science fiction. No one today, however, questions the possibility of such an identification process.

In a final act of rebellion against God, this vile person will set himself up in Jerusalem and desecrate the rebuilt temple in what is called the "abomination of desolation" (Matthew 24:15). He will then attempt to annihilate every Jew on earth, thus sounding the first ominous note in the prelude to the Battle of Armageddon. This despot of all despots will be ultimately destroyed when Jesus Christ comes to battle against the Antichrist and his armies. In that climactic war, the Antichrist will be killed, and his forces will be destroyed. The victorious Christ will assume His throne as rightful king and ruler of the universe.

Is the Antichrist lurking somewhere out there in the masses of humanity right now? Is his darkened mind already plotting the evils that he will inflict in the last days? I believe it is entirely possible, if not highly probable.

REMEMBER: Satan, the power broker behind the rise of the Antichrist, is not all-powerful or all-knowing. Like us, he is looking for the signs and waiting.

A NEW AXIS OF EVIL

Prophetic Connection: *The book of Ezekiel describes a future union between nation states focused on the destruction of Israel.*

On January 29, 2002, in his State of the Union address—the first State of the Union after the horrific events of September 11, 2001—President George W. Bush used the term *Axis of Evil* for the first time. He identified Iran, Iraq, and North Korea as "states . . . [who are] arming to threaten the peace of the world. . . . These regimes," he said, "pose a grave threat and growing danger. They could provide these arms to terrorists, giving them the means to match their hatred."[1] At the time, President Bush was roundly criticized for calling these nations evil, but as we will see, his description was accurate, at least in part.

One nation on this Axis of Evil list is of special interest to us because it is also on God's list. That nation and that list are found in the thirty-eighth and thirty-ninth chapters of Ezekiel. These chapters, written some twenty-six hundred years ago, give us one of the most important and dramatic prophecies in all Scripture.

This is commonly referred to as the prophecy against

Gog and Magog, and it is the most detailed prophecy concerning war in the entire Bible. The prophecy predicts an invasion of Israel in the last days—an invasion comprised of enormous masses of troops from a coalition of nations led by Russia and Iran.

It is likely that this invasion will occur shortly after Israel signs a covenant with the new leader of the European Union. Because of this agreement, Israel will be at peace with her Islamic neighbors. The people of Israel will believe that the European powers will protect them from any outside aggressor or invader . . . especially from Russia, which will have joined forces with Iran to develop weapons for the purpose of utterly destroying Israel.

This will be a dark moment in the prophetic timetable, but it will also mark the beginning of evil's last stand. The battle will belong to the Lord, and in the end the kingdom of God will be established on the earth!

REMEMBER: Though the world tends to dismiss the very notion of evil, the Bible and our own experience confirms its existence. When evil is wielded by nations backed by demonic forces, it can do tremendous damage.

THE LEADERS OF THE GREAT BATTLE

Prophetic Connection: *Scripture warns that Gog (a ruler) and Magog (a nation) will lead the future coalition seeking the destruction of Israel.*

Ezekiel's prophecy in Ezekiel 38–39 begins with a list of proper names. Many of these names identify certain grandchildren and greatgrandchildren of Noah who were the fathers of nations that for a time bore their names (Genesis 10). These nations, which today no longer have those original names, will ultimately form a coalition that will march against Israel. As we identify these nations by their present names and locate them on today's world map, we can see how the stage is being set for a Russian-Islamic invasion of Israel.

Gog is an exception on Ezekiel's list. Gog is not one of the descendants of Noah listed in Genesis 10. That name, however, is found twelve times in Ezekiel 38–39. It is not the name of a nation, but rather the title of a ruler. In fact, the word means "ruler," or "the man on top." It is clear that Gog is an individual rather than a nation because God addresses him as such in this prophecy (see Ezekiel 38:14; 39:1). Furthermore, Gog is explicitly called "the prince" in Ezekiel 38:2 and 39:1.

The next name in Ezekiel's prophecy is Magog. In his book *The Nations in Prophecy*, John F. Walvoord wrote, "Magog is best identified with the Scythians. . . . The ancient historian Josephus makes that identification, and we have no reason to question it. The Scythians apparently lived immediately to the north of . . . Israel, then some of them emigrated north, going all the way to the Asiatic Circle."[1]

Interestingly, Herodotus records that these Scythians were of Indo-Aryan heritage and spoke an Iranian language related to Persian.[2] Using these clues, we can identify Magog today as being made up of nations that were formerly parts of the Soviet Union: Kazakhstan, Kyrgyzstan, Uzbekistan, Turkmenistan, Tajikistan, Azerbaijan, Georgia, and possibly Afghanistan.

Though the names of places change over time, the Bible is completely accurate in the prophecies it contains. The map of the world today looks very different than it did in Ezekiel's day, but God has not lost track of any people group, and He knows precisely who will come against the people of Israel in the future. For that reason, we would be wise to pay attention to world events as we study the Scriptures.

REMEMBER: "Whoever blesses Israel will be blessed, and whoever curses Israel will be cursed" (Numbers 24:9 GNT).

THE NATION FROM THE NORTH

Prophetic Connection: *Scripture helps us identify "Rosh" as a key member of the future coalition that will seek to destroy Israel.*

The next name on Ezekiel's list is Rosh, which is found in the Old Testament more than six hundred times. During Ezekiel's time, the word *Rosh* identified a nation that included people living north of the Black Sea. In the prophecies of Ezekiel, we are told three times (38:6, 15; 39:2) that part of the force that invades Israel will come from the "distant north," or "the remotest parts of the north." The land that is most distantly north and remote to Israel is Russia.

John F. Walvoord wrote:

> If one takes any map of the world and draws a line north of the land of Israel he will inevitably come to the nation of Russia. As soon as the line is drawn to the far north beyond Asia Minor and the Black Sea it is in Russia and continues to be Russia for many hundreds of miles all the way to the Arctic Circle. . . . On the basis of geography alone, it seems quite clear that the only nation which could possibly

be referred to as coming from the far north would be the nation of Russia.[1]

When the Soviet Union collapsed in the 1990s, many people thought Russia's days of prominence and power were over. But just a few decades later, we find a resurgent Russia seeking to reclaim the strategic ground she lost. Someone has said that since the days of the collapse of the Soviet Union, the great Russian bear has been like a mother bear robbed of her cubs.[2] If Magog includes the countries of the collapsed Soviet Union, Rosh specifically identifies the nation of Russia, which is presently trying to reassemble its lost empire.

Edward Lucas, a journalist who has covered Eastern Europe for *The Economist* for more than twenty years, wrote a frightening book titled *The New Cold War*. He warns that Russia is rising again as a hostile power. It is reasserting its military muscle, intensely pursuing global energy markets, coercing neighboring nations back into the old Soviet orbit, silencing journalists and dissidents, and laying the groundwork with modernized weaponry for reestablishing its former power and influence. The West, wrote Lucas, is asleep to the growing danger and is losing the New Cold War.[3] This analysis serves as a reminder that we must be ever watchful, paying close attention to the changing political realities in our world. As the prophetic pieces fall into place according to God's Word, we can be confident Christ's return is not far behind.

REMEMBER: There is no geopolitical change that will avert the battle described in Ezekiel 38–39. While we must certainly pray for peace, ultimately peace will only come when the Prince of Peace returns.

PERSIA'S POWER

Prophetic Connection: *Scripture offers helpful insight on Iran's current and future plans to wipe Israel off the map.*

Perhaps the most easily identifiable nation on Ezekiel's list is Persia, a name that appears thirty times in the Old Testament. Persia retained its ancient name until March 1935, when it became the nation of Iran. Today, with its population of eighty-seven million people, Iran has become the hotbed of militant Islam and anti-Semitic hatred.

Iran's government is officially a theocratic republic whose ultimate political authority resides in the supreme leader, currently Ayatollah Ali Khamenei. Iran's geographical location on the Persian Gulf and the vital Strait of Hormuz gives her great power. Iran is identified as a prime player in the human trafficking trade. It is also a "key transshipment point" for heroin into Europe.[1] Additionally, the United States has identified Iran as a state sponsor of terrorism.

The Iranian regime is well known for its hatred of Israel and its desire to eliminate her. In October 2005, then newly elected president Mahmoud Ahmadinejad declared to the World Without Zionism audience, "As the imam said, Israel must be wiped off the map. . . . Anybody who recognizes Israel will burn in the fire of the Islamic nation's fury."[2]

Hezbollah is an Islamic fundamentalist group, and though its base of operations is Lebanon, its authority comes from a source higher in the Islamic hierarchy. In this case the ruling jurisprudent would again be the supreme leader of Iran—Ayatollah Khamenei. "We ask, receive answers, and then apply. This is even true for acts of suicide for the sake of Allah—no one may kill himself without a jurisprudence permission [from Khamenei]."[3] Thus we can see that the aggressive and threatening influence of Iran infects and controls other Islamic terrorist organizations.

Iran's utter disdain for world opinion is pretty convincing evidence that our national leaders are right on target in including Iran as a member of the Axis of Evil—and that Ezekiel's prophecy concerning Persia is spot-on.

REMEMBER: The great battle at the end of history will be the culmination of all that's come before. Persia may have become Iran, but the nation's opposition to Israel has not changed.

GOMER'S GREAT ARMY

Prophetic Connection: *The modern nation of Turkey will be another player in the future war against Israel.*

Another prominent name on Ezekiel's list is Gomer, which many Bible readers struggle to identify. Gomer is mentioned in Genesis 10 as one of Japheth's sons. Genesis 10:3 helps us further by telling us that one of Gomer's relatives is Ashkenaz. Today, Israelis describe Jews from Germany, Austria, and Poland as *Ashkenazim*. This gives us a clue to Gomer's present-day identity, as this term has likely been passed down through generations, retaining the identity of the people even as the name of the countries have changed. Edward Gibbon, in *The History of the Decline and Fall of the Roman Empire*, tells us, "Gomer is modern Germany."[1] The modern nation identified as the ancient land of Gomer is usually thought to be either Germany or Turkey.

Ezekiel 38:6 refers to Gomer with "all its troops" (NKJV), or "all his bands" (KJV), or "all his hordes" (ASV), indicating that this nation will provide a powerful army in the assault on Israel. If ancient Gomer is part of modern Turkey, as I believe it to be, it is a country with a growing allegiance to Russia. If we listen to the news, we know this nation has a strong military presence on the northern border of Iraq—quite possibly the "hordes" that Ezekiel refers to—and has already been involved in the conflict over the control of the Middle East.

You may be asking, "Why is the identification of these nations so important to us?" After all, whatever is going to happen *will* happen, whether or not we're able to pin these ancient nations on a modern map. The answer is that, as the pieces of Ezekiel's prophecy fall into place, the Bible's perfect testimony is reinforced. For believers, that means increased faith and encouragement as we continue on in this world of trouble. For non-believers, the veracity of the Bible opens a door to faith in Jesus Christ.

REMEMBER: "See then that you walk circumspectly, not as fools but as wise, redeeming the time, because the days are evil" (Ephesians 5:15–16).

SEEING IS BELIEVING

Prophetic Connection: *We can see biblical prophecies coming true today just by reading the news.*

Reviewing Ezekiel's list of nations that will come against Israel in the last days is eye-opening. What a formidable list it is! Nearly all of these nations are either Islamic or pro-Islamic. When this formidable mass of armies comes against Israel, there will be no possible human defense for the Israelis.

In a verse that follows this prophecy, Ezekiel spoke of some nations that will not be involved in the invasion of Israel: "Sheba, Dedan, the merchants of Tarshish, and all their young lions will say to you, 'Have you come to take plunder? Have you gathered your army to take booty, to carry away silver and gold, to take away livestock and goods, to take great plunder?'" (38:13). Most Bible scholars believe that Sheba and Dedan refer to the people of the Arabian Peninsula, including modern-day Saudi Arabia, Yemen, Oman, and the Gulf countries of Kuwait and the United Arab Emirates.

Tarshish was a term that in ancient times described the westernmost part of human civilization. Many scholars believe that "the merchants of Tarshish" and its "villages" and "young lions" refer to the market-based economies of Western Europe. Some scholars have even dared to be more specific. Dr. David L. Cooper wrote, "When all the historical statements are examined thoroughly, it seems that the evidence is in favor of identifying Tarshish as England."[1] Another scholar, Theodore Epp, agrees with this identification. He points out that the lion is a symbol for Britain and suggests that Britain's colonies, many of which have spun off to become nations of their own, are the cubs, or "young lions" in Ezekiel's prophecy. He said, "Great Britain's young lions, such as Canada, Australia, New Zealand, the African colonies, and the United States are strong enough to make an exhibit of disfavor in that day."[2]

If Theodore Epp and Dr. Cooper are right, it seems that the West in general will not participate in the invasion of Israel. What interests us is that Ezekiel's prophecy of the alignment of nations, showing which ones will and which will not rise to crush Israel, squares very closely with the alignment of nations we see shaping up in the world right now. Thus, we find that Ezekiel's ancient prophecy, written some twenty-six hundred years ago, informs us as to what is going on in the world today right before our very eyes.

REMEMBER: The Bible is unique in that it is the only book in which ancient prophecies give specific details about events that are unfolding in modern times. Only the true God of the universe could be so accurate!

A LAND OF UNWALLED VILLAGES

Prophetic Connection: *Israel will believe itself to be at peace when the great battle occurs, but that peace will be shattered.*

Ezekiel clearly identifies Israel as the land that will be invaded by the nations described in Ezekiel 38. He stresses this fact at least five times in the chapter—sometimes obliquely, giving us some characteristic of the people to be invaded, and sometimes explicitly, identifying the land by name:

> "You will come into the land of those brought back from the sword and gathered from many people on the mountains of Israel, which had long been desolate; they were brought out of the nations, and now all of them dwell safely. . . . 'a land of unwalled villages; I will go to a peaceful people, who dwell safely, all of them dwelling without walls, and having neither bars nor gates' . . . a people gathered from the nations. . . . '"On that day when My people Israel dwell safely. . . . You will come up against my people Israel.'" (vv. 8, 11, 12, 14, 16)

The prophet tells us that the invasion of Israel will take place sometime in the future—"In the latter years" (v. 8). It will happen at a time when Israel is dwelling in peace and safety and not involved in conflict with other nations.

Has there ever been such a time in Israel's history? No, there has not! Is today such a time? No! When will there be such a time? The only period in Israel's life likely to meet this requirement will come immediately following the Rapture of the church when the Antichrist and the European Union make a treaty with Israel to guarantee her peace and security. When this treaty is signed, the people of Israel will relax the diligence they have been forced to maintain since the modern founding of their nation in 1948. They will rely on the treaty and turn their attention away from defense to concentrate on increasing their wealth.

Israel will truly be a land of unwalled villages. Her defenses will be down, and she will be woefully unprepared for the invasion by the armies of Russia and the coalition. The coming invasion of Israel will be something of a perfect storm—an unprepared nation believing they are at peace with the world will face an insurmountable coalition of nations bent on her destruction.

REMEMBER: "And it shall happen in that day that I will make Jerusalem a very heavy stone for all peoples; all who would heave it away will surely be cut in pieces, though all nations of the earth are gathered against it" (Zechariah 12:3).

THE SPOILS OF WAR

Prophetic Connection: *Biblical prophecy helps us understand why so many nations will join forces for the future invasion of Israel.*

The nations in the Battle of Gog and Magog will come down on the nation of Israel, pursuing three primary goals. The first goal will be to seize her land. As Ezekiel put it, "to stretch out your hand against the waste places that are again inhabited" (Ezekiel 38:12). The second goal of the invaders will be to steal Israel's wealth: "to take plunder and to take booty, to stretch out your hand . . . against a people gathered from the nations, who have acquired livestock and goods, who dwell in the midst of the land. . . . To carry away silver and gold, to take away livestock and goods, to take great plunder" (vv. 12–13).

There is plenty of wealth to be plundered in modern Israel, as we can see by the following quote from a 2007 article in the *Jerusalem Post*: "Despite a population of only slightly more than 7 million people . . . Israel is now home to more than 7,200 millionaires. . . . Of the 500 wealthiest people in the world, six are now Israeli, and all told, Israel's rich had assets in 2007 of more than 35 billion dollars. . . .

Israel's GDP is almost double that of any other Middle East country."[1]

According to one prosperity index, Israel exported goods and services of more than $70 billion last year, including $34.2 billion from the technology sector alone. "Israel is the highest-ranking Middle Eastern country in the index."[2] In 2023, she had a per capita gross domestic product index of $52,000, which compared favorably with the much larger European Union at $60,000.[3] Any way you measure it, Israel has become prosperous, and despite a recent recession and military conflict, her economy has continued to grow.

Finally, the invading nations have as their ultimate goal the wholesale slaughter of Israel's people: "I will go to a peaceful people, who dwell safely, all of them dwelling without walls, and having neither bars nor gates . . . to stretch out your hand . . . against a people gathered from the nations. . . . You will come up against My people Israel like a cloud, to cover the land" (vv. 11–12, 16). The historical accumulated hatred for the Jews will drive these armies forward with the assurance that this time, the people of Israel will not escape death.

REMEMBER: In the dark moments of war, it will appear that evil has triumphed. But it seemed that way on Good Friday, too.

DIVINE INTERVENTION

Prophetic Connection: *When all seems lost for God's chosen people, He will step in to fight for Israel once again.*

When the massive Russian-Islamic armies assemble on the northern mountains of Israel, ready to come against that tiny country, it will appear to be the most grossly mismatched contest in military history. The Israelis will be so outnumbered that there will be no human way they can win this war. Only intervention by God Himself could possibly save them. And that is exactly what will happen.

When God goes to war, He uses weapons unique to Him—weapons that render the arsenals of men as ineffective as a water pistol against a nuclear bomb. God will save His people Israel by employing four of these weapons simultaneously. First, he will rout the armies of Israel's attackers with massive convulsions in the earth. As Ezekiel explains: "The mountains shall be thrown down, the steep places shall fall, and every wall shall fall to the ground" (38:20).

God will follow these convulsions of the earth with His second weapon, which will be to create such confusion among the attacking troops that they will panic and begin killing one another: "'I will call for a sword against Gog throughout all My mountains,' says the LORD God. 'Every man's sword shall be against his brother'" (v. 21). Many soldiers will die in the divinely imposed bewilderment, largely by what today we would call "friendly fire."

The third divine weapon will be the contagion of disease: "And I will bring him to judgment with pestilence and bloodshed," asserts the Lord (v. 22). He will infect the invading troops with some debilitating disease that will render them incapable of carrying out an effective attack. God will follow this contagion with his fourth and final weapon: calamities from the sky. "I will rain down on him, on his troops, and on the many peoples who are with him, flooding rain, great hailstones, fire, and brimstone" (v. 22).

One man has written: "Every force of nature is a servant of the Living God, and in a moment can be made a soldier, armed to the teeth. Men are slowly discovering that God's forces stored in nature are mightier than the brawn of the human arm."[1] When God goes to war, no army on earth can stand against His formidable arsenal. The armies that come against Israel in the last days will learn that truth the hard way.

REMEMBER: "Who is this King of glory? The LORD strong and mighty, the LORD mighty in battle" (Psalm 24:8).

ANOTHER DISPLAY OF SOVEREIGNTY

Prophetic Connection: *We can see hints of God's plans and purposes for allowing (and even initiating) this future battle against Israel.*

To understand what is going on in the war and destruction described in Ezekiel's prophecy, we must first consider the sovereignty of God's plan. We have already observed that even in the most devastating of times, God is still in control. In fact, He often orchestrates events to bring about His purposes. He tells us what He will do to Israel's enemies in no uncertain terms: "I will turn you around, put hooks into your jaws, and lead you out, with all your army, horses, and horsemen" (Ezekiel 38:4); "It will be in the latter days that I will bring you against My land" (v. 16); "and I will turn you around and lead you on, bringing you up from the far north, and bring you against the mountains of Israel" (39:2).

Passages such as these confuse many people because of the seeming implication that God leads men to be evil or to do evil things. But the Bible never says that God instills evil in the hearts of men. Even though men try to thwart His plans and wreak great destruction, God's purpose will always win out. When Ezekiel wrote that God will bring the enemy against His land, he was simply saying that God will bring these nations to the doom that their wickedness inevitably demands. Everyone accomplishes God's will in the end. Those who conform to His will accomplish it willingly; those who do not conform accomplish it inadvertently as an unwitting tool in His hands.

But why will God allow Israel to be invaded in the first place? What good will come from it? God tells us: "I will set My glory among the nations; all the nations shall see My judgment which I have executed, and My hand which I have laid on them. So, the house of Israel shall know that I am the LORD their God from that day forward (39:21–22; see also 38:16, 23; 39:6–7).

It doesn't take a rocket scientist to figure out God's purpose in the cataclysmic battle of the last days. It is clear and simple. God intends for people to recognize Him as the Lord God of heaven, whose name is holy, whose glory fills the universe, and whom men must recognize as sovereign if they are to find the peace and joy He desires for His people.

REMEMBER: "And we know that all things work together for good to those who love God, to those who are the called according to His purpose" (Romans 8:28).

TAKE A LOOK INSIDE

Prophetic Connection: *Biblical prophecy reveals the reality of evil in our world, present and future. Scripture also shows us how to deal with the evil in our own hearts.*

No matter how great the evil in men's hearts, no matter how much destruction and death that evil brings about, God's ultimate purpose in confronting evil, in revealing His glory among the nations, and in bringing His own from the lands of the enemy is always to accomplish the salvation of His people.

As Ezekiel shows us so vividly, God's destruction of the Axis of Evil in the last days will accomplish the salvation of his people, the nation of Israel. By identifying this Axis of Evil as modern nations who are unwittingly bent on fulfilling this devastating prophecy, we have shown how present events will lead to the ultimate accomplishment of God's good purposes. We have also demonstrated that the growing darkness spreading all around us will not have the final word.

Of course, there is also the potential for an axis of evil within the heart of each person. As the apostle Paul tells us, each of us possesses that "sinful nature" we inherited from Adam—a propensity for selfish evil that, if not controlled by the presence of God's Spirit, can run rampant and produce destruction in our own lives and in the lives of those about us.

But thanks be to God, His salvation is not for Israel only. All men and women today can choose to be among God's people. You don't have to be a Jew to receive salvation, nor does being a Russian or an Iranian force one to be a part of the Axis of Evil. God in His infinite love pours out His Spirit on all who believe and turn to Him. Through that wonderful transaction, and as His Spirit is poured out on the redeemed, the axis of evil in our hearts is transformed by God's love.

REMEMBER: "For if you live according to the flesh you will die; but if by the Spirit you put to death the deeds of the body, you will live" (Romans 8:13)."

ARMAGEDDON

Prophetic Connection: *The Bible describes a "war to end all wars" that will occur at the end of the Tribulation.*

Armageddon. The very word chills the soul. Probably there are few adults who are not familiar with that word and what it implies. But have you noticed that our national leaders in the twentieth and twenty-first centuries began regularly using that doomsday word in their speaking and writing? They warn about financial Armageddon if this policy or that policy is adopted into law. They warn about climate Armageddon if certain environmental benchmarks aren't reached for cutting CO_2. They warn about destructive Armageddon if certain nations are allowed to pursue nuclear weapons (or if advanced nations fail to disarm).

Why the sudden embrace of that particular term? I believe it is because they can see how modern weaponry and international tensions reveal how quickly global equilibrium could get out of control, leading to a cataclysmic war such as the world has never seen before.

Our nation is no stranger to war. The United States has officially declared war eleven times and has been involved in more than one hundred military conflicts. This averages out to one war or conflict for every two years of America's history. This number includes not only the major conflicts, but also lesser-known engagements such as the Seminole Wars, America's involvement in the Boxer Rebellion, and the invasion of Panama. Approximately 1.3 million troops have died for their country in these wars.

The Bible tells us there is yet another war to be fought on this earth. This war, called Armageddon, makes all the wars America has fought to date look like minor skirmishes. It will be unlike anything the world has ever seen. This war will draw the final curtain on modern civilization.

Believe it or not, preparations for that war are underway right now throughout the world, even if political powers and parliaments don't quite realize what they're doing. The only thing holding back Armageddon's rapid approach is the yet-to-occur disappearance of all true believers in Jesus Christ, the event we know as the Rapture of the church. When the saints are taken away, evil will multiply, and then nothing will be able to hold back the deadliest of wars.

REMEMBER: Like the people in Noah's day, we tend to believe the world will simply go on forever, but the Rapture, and then Armageddon, will change everything. Now is the time to come to Christ and be saved!

SETTING THE STAGE

Prophetic Connection: *Scripture reveals many of the events and motivations that will drive the world toward the final, climactic battle we call Armageddon.*

In the twelfth chapter of Revelation, the apostle John revealed how Armageddon will come about. "So the great dragon was cast out, that serpent of old, called the Devil and Satan, who deceives the whole world; he was cast to the earth, and his angels were cast out with him. . . . Now when the dragon saw that he had been cast to the earth, he persecuted the woman who gave birth to the male Child" (vv. 9, 13).

These verses tell us that during the Tribulation, Satan will persecute the woman who brought forth the male child. This "woman" is an obvious metaphor for Israel, through whom the child Jesus was born. Satan's first attempt at persecution will be the Battle of Gog and Magog. As we have seen, this battle, which precedes the Battle of Armageddon, will involve a massive, Russia-led coalition of nations coming against Israel like swarms of hornets against a defenseless child. As Revelation tells us, Satan will be the motivating force behind this invasion. But before he accomplishes his intended annihilation of Israel, she will be rescued by Almighty God.

The thwarting at the Battle of Gog and Magog will be a setback to Satan, but he will not give up; he will be relentless in his persecution of the Jews. His purpose, beginning in the middle of the Tribulation period, will be to destroy the Jewish people before Christ can set up His kingdom, thus wrecking God's prophesied rule over the earth during the Millennium.

According to Revelation 16, Satan will employ two fearful personalities to join him in these plans: "And I saw three unclean spirits like frogs coming out of the mouth of the dragon, out of the mouth of the beast, and out of the mouth of the false prophet" (v. 13). Here John tells us that Satan will empower the beast, the head of the reestablished Roman Empire, and the false prophet, the head of the new world religious system. Thus Satan (the dragon), the Beast (the Antichrist), and the false prophet become the unholy trinity committed to the destruction of Israel. When the church of Jesus Christ is taken safely into heaven and the Tribulation period begins, the unrestrained satanic persecution of Israel will propel the entire world toward the Battle of Armageddon.

REMEMBER: In the days leading up to the Battle of Armageddon, Satan will be pulling the strings of his servants, the Antichrist and the false prophet. But be aware—the devil is at work even today, manipulating current events in an attempt to thwart God's plans.

THE MOST NATURAL BATTLEGROUND ON THE WHOLE EARTH

Prophetic Connection: *The primary location in which the Battle of Armageddon will occur has a rich history in God's Word.*

The word *Armageddon* is much bandied about these days. It has become a synonym for every kind of dooms-day scenario. But Armageddon is not actually a battle; it is a place. Given the enormous attention this word receives, it may surprise you that Armageddon is mentioned only once in the Bible—in Revelation 16:16.

The Hebrew word *harmageddon* means "the mount of Megiddo." *Har* means mount, and *megiddo* means slaughter; so the meaning of Armageddon is "Mount of Slaughter." While the word *Armageddon* is mentioned only once in the Bible, the mountain of Megiddo has a rich biblical history. It was at Megiddo that Deborah and Barak defeated the Canaanites (Judges 4–5). It was also there that Gideon defeated the Midianites (Judges 7), Saul was slain during a war with the Philistines (1 Samuel 31), Ahaziah was slain by Jehu (2 Kings 9), and Josiah was slain by the invading Egyptians (2 Kings 23).

The Crusaders, the Egyptians, the Persians, the Druze, the Greeks, the Turks, the Arabs, and others have all fought there at one time or another. As you can see, Megiddo has earned its awful name: it is indeed a Mount of Slaughter. Napoleon once said of the place: "All the armies of the world could maneuver their forces on this vast plain. . . . There is no place in the whole world more suited for war than this. . . . [It is] the most natural battleground on the whole earth."[1]

While the battle we call Armageddon will be centralized on that field, it will not be contained there. All the ancient prophets agree that this war will be fought throughout the entire land of Israel. The words of the prophet Zechariah reveal Jerusalem will be at the center of conflict during the Armageddon war. "Behold, I will make Jerusalem a cup of drunkenness to all the surrounding peoples, when they lay siege against Judah and Jerusalem" (Zechariah 12:2).

This war will be horrific. The Bible says blood will flow in staggering torrents—"up to the horses' bridles, for one thousand six hundred furlongs" (Revelation 14:20). That many furlongs translates into almost exactly two hundred miles.

REMEMBER: Though the destruction wrought by the Armageddon campaign will be great, there will come a peace and a victory far greater. In the midst of the darkest storms, we must keep our eyes fixed on Jesus, our only hope.

A THREEFOLD JUDGMENT

Prophetic Connection: *The Bible reveals three reasons why God will initiate the Battle of Armageddon at the end of the Tribulation.*

Our sensibilities revolt when we read about the carnage the Bible pictures when describing the Battle of Armageddon. For example: "Then I saw an angel standing in the sun; and he cried with a loud voice, saying to all the birds that fly in the midst of heaven, 'Come and gather together for the supper of the great God, that you may eat the flesh of kings, the flesh of captains, the flesh of mighty men, the flesh of horses and of those who sit on them, and the flesh of all *people,* free and slave, both small and great" (Rev. 19:17–18).

Such a horrible scene raises the question: What is the purpose of this war in the plan of God?

There are actually three purposes in the mind of God concerning the Battle of Armageddon. First, the battle will complete His judgment upon Israel. The Tribulation will be a time of divine indignation against the people of Israel, the people who rejected their Messiah and—time and time again after given the chance to return—failed to heed the corrective and punitive judgment of God. It is no accident that this future period of time is often referred to as "the time of Jacob's trouble" (Jeremiah 30:7).

Second, God will finalize His judgment upon the nations that have persecuted Israel. Those nations will be gathered together in the Battle of Armageddon, in the Valley of Jehoshaphat, giving God the perfect opportunity to deal with them finally and decisively (Joel 3:2).

Finally, God will use Armageddon to formally judge all the nations that have rejected Him. "Now out of His mouth goes a sharp sword, that with it He should strike the nations. And He Himself will rule them with a rod of iron. He Himself treads the winepress of the fierceness and wrath of Almighty God" (Revelation 19:15).

To our time-bound senses, God's activity often seems so slow and ponderous that people pursuing ungodly goals tend to dismiss His judgment as a factor to be taken lightly. Thus the nations do not believe a time is coming when God's judgment will inevitably descend. But be assured, He is storing up judgment against a day to come. The Bible is clear: one of these days God will have enough, and His judgment will pour down like consuming fire against the world's wicked nations.

REMEMBER: Judgment is coming for all those who have refused Christ's sacrifice. However, God has done everything to save people: "For God did not send His Son into the world to condemn the world, but that the world through Him might be saved" (John 3:17).

THE TREATY BEFORE THE WAR

Prophetic Connection: *Even during the terror of the Tribulation, many will be motivated by seeking peace rather than war.*

Just to be sure there is no confusion about the wars during the Tribulation period, it's important to remember we have identified two separate battles. There is the first battle, the one that will occur at the beginning of the Tribulation period when Gog (Russia) assembles a mass of nations against Israel and is thwarted by God's intervention. Then there is a second battle, one that will end the Tribulation period. It is easy to confuse the two, but the Bible presents them as two distinct events, separated by several years and involving different participants.

All the nations of the world will be involved in the Battle of Armageddon, and they will be led by the Antichrist. But the Bible gives us many more details about the motives and actions of the participants in this battle. These are worth exploring, as they provide insights into the nature of the war and why it will be fought.

Referring specifically to the Antichrist, Daniel tells us

that "he shall confirm a covenant with many for one week" (Daniel 9:27). In prophetic language, this means a week of years, so the covenant will be made for seven years. Apparently in the last days, Israel will be so wearied of continual threats of war that they will think any treaty, even one that gives them a short space of breathing room, will be better than no peace at all.

The Antichrist, who will at this time be the head of the European Union, will sign such a covenant with Israel, guaranteeing peace and security for seven years. Israel will view this man not as the evil Antichrist but as a beneficent and charismatic leader.

On the heels of the covenant with Israel, this self-appointed world ruler will begin to strengthen his power by performing amazing signs and wonders, including even a supposed resurrection from the dead (Revelation 13:3). Then, with his grip on the world greatly enhanced, he will boldly take the next step in his arrogant defiance of God: "Then the king shall do according to his own will: he shall exalt and magnify himself above every god, shall speak blasphemies against the God of gods" (Daniel 11:36). In this way, the Antichrist will reveal who he really is—but by that point, it will be too late. His grip on power will be fierce, and his aims diabolical.

REMEMBER: There is no lasting peace except that which the Prince of Peace brings.

THE DICTATOR FROM HELL

Prophetic Connection: *The Antichrist's rise to power will mirror that of many dictators from history, but with much greater consequences.*

The Antichrist will be the epitome of the man with a compulsion to extend his dominion over everything and everyone. To achieve this end, the Antichrist will bow to no god but the "god of fortresses" (Daniel 11:38). That is, he will build enormous military might and engage in extensive warfare to extend his power throughout the world.

Daniel 11:36 describes how the swollen megalomania of the Antichrist will drive him to take his next step. John expands on Daniel's description of the Antichrist's blasphemous acts by telling us that every living person will be required to worship this man. "He was granted power to give breath to the image of the beast, that the image of the beast should both speak and cause as many as would not worship the image of the beast to be killed" (Revelation 13:15). Step by step, the Antichrist will promote himself from a European leader, to a world leader, to a tyrannical global dictator, and finally to a god.

The Antichrist's grip on global power will not last long,

however. The world will become increasingly discontented with the leadership of this global dictator. Major segments of the world will begin to assemble their own military forces and rebel against him. "At the time of the end the king of the South shall attack him; and the king of the North shall come against him like a whirlwind, with chariots, horsemen, and with many ships" (Daniel 11:40).

John Walvoord pinpoints the source of this army and describes the magnitude of the initial thrust against the Antichrist:

> Daniel's prophecy described a great army from Africa, including not only Egypt but other countries of that continent. This army, probably numbering in the millions, will attack the Middle East from the south. At the same time Russia and the other armies to the north will mobilize another powerful military force to descend on the Holy Land and challenge the world dictator. Although Russia will have had a severe setback about four years earlier in the prophetic sequence of events, she apparently will have been able to recoup her losses enough to put another army in the field.[1]

The Antichrist will put down some of these first attempts at rebellion against him. But before he can celebrate and move on toward his goal of destroying Israel and Jerusalem, something almost unthinkable will happen. . . .

REMEMBER: Even with the power of Satan behind him, the Antichrist will not be able to escape the consequences of his broken promises. Just as it is now, the truth of God's Word will be the only truth to stand upon.

ALL DRIED UP

Prophetic Connection: *The Antichrist will suffer a setback when the Euphrates River dries up, making a way for his enemies to advance.*

The Bible leaves no doubt as to the event that will so disturb and enrage the Antichrist: "Then the sixth angel poured out his bowl on the great river Euphrates, and its water was dried up, so that the way of the kings from the east might be prepared" (Revelation 16:12).

The Euphrates is one of the greatest rivers in the world. It flows from the mountains of western Turkey, through Syria, and continues right through the heart of Iraq, not far from Baghdad. It eventually unites with the Tigris to become the *Shatt el Arab*, and finally empties into the Persian Gulf.

What is the significance of the drying up of the Euphrates River, and why will that event have such a disturbing effect on the Antichrist? For an explanation, let's turn to John Walvoord:

> The drying-up of the Euphrates is a prelude to the final act of the drama, not the act itself. We must conclude, then, that the most probable interpretation of the drying-up

of the Euphrates is that by an act of God its flow will be interrupted even as were the waters of the Red Sea and of Jordan. This time the way will open not for Israel but for those who are referred to as the Kings of the East.[1]

It's no wonder the world dictator will be disturbed and frustrated. He will have just put down rebellions by defeating armies from the south and the north, and just as it appears he is about to gain control of everything, he will get word that the Euphrates River has dried up and massive armies of the east are crossing it to come against him. Having thought himself safe, as no army could cross this barrier and come into the Israeli arena, he will receive word that an army of unprecedented numbers is marching toward him.

When this unprecedented army of two hundred million soldiers (Revelation 9:16) crosses the bed of the Euphrates against the Antichrist, the greatest war of all history will be set in motion.

REMEMBER: The same God who parted the sea (Exodus 14:21–29) and calmed the storm (Mark 4:35–41) will dry up one of the world's mightiest rivers in the last days.

A DEMONIC WAR

Prophetic Connection: *Scripture helps us see the spiritual foundations of end-times events, including the Battle of Armageddon.*

When we think about future events, there is an easy temptation to see them in a similar vein as current events. Meaning, we think most about people and nations and treaties and military advances and so on. We forget to think about the supernatural elements that are always present behind those events.

The apostle John tells us that all these events leading up to the Battle of Armageddon will be inspired and directed by the demons of hell: "For they are spirits of demons, performing signs, which go out to the kings of the earth and of the whole world, to gather them to the battle of that great day of God Almighty" (Revelation 16:14).

> No doubt demonism in every shape and form will manifest itself more and more as the end draws near, until at last it all ends in Armageddon. . . . But besides these hosts of human armies, there will also be present at Armageddon an innumerable host of supernatural beings. . . . So

Armageddon will truly be a battle of heaven and earth and hell.[1]

Of course, this should not surprise us. Even in our day, the battles we face are spiritual in nature, even though the battles themselves play out in the natural realm here on earth. As Paul told the believers in Ephesus, "For we do not wrestle against flesh and blood, but against principalities, against powers, against the rulers of the darkness of this age, against spiritual hosts of wickedness in the heavenly places" (Ephesians 6:12). It is these same principalities and powers who will instigate events in the last days.

What we see in Revelation is the culmination of the rebellion that began long ago in Eden when the serpent, later identified as Satan, tempted and deceived our first parents, bringing sin into the world in an attempt to thwart God's good plans for His creation. The Son of God came into the world to destroy the works of the devil (1 John 3:8)—and on the cross, He silenced the accuser's hellish accusations. Even so, the powers of darkness have not ceased in their rebellion, and as history edges closer and closer to its conclusion, their wickedness will be revealed for all to see.

REMEMBER: There is more taking place than what we can see with our natural eyes. The spiritual powers of darkness seek to influence political rulers and entire nations. That is why we must remain close to Christ in all things—so that we are not deceived.

THE RETURN OF THE KING

Prophetic Connection: *Christ's physical return will be the beginning of the end for the terrible battle we call Armageddon.*

We've learned much about the coming Battle of Armageddon in recent days—the players involved, their motivations, and the chaos that is to come. If you are a follower of Christ, what happens next during the Battle of Armageddon may instill an urge to stand up and shout like a football fan watching the star quarterback come onto the field.

> Now I saw heaven opened, and behold, a white horse. And He who sat on him was called Faithful and True, and in righteousness He judges and makes war. His eyes were like a flame of fire, and on His head were many crowns. . . . And the armies in heaven, clothed in fine linen, white and clean, followed Him on white horses. Now out of His mouth goes a sharp sword, that with it He should strike the nations. . . . And He has on His robe and on His thigh a name written: KING OF KINGS AND LORD OF LORDS. (Revelation 19:11–12, 14–16)

The great Lord Jesus—the captain of the Lord's hosts, the King over all kings—will descend to defend and protect

His chosen people and put a once-and-for-all end to the evil of the Antichrist. But the Lord Jesus will not descend alone. "Behold, the Lord comes with ten thousands of His saints" (Jude 14).

All those who have died in the Lord, along with those who were raptured before the years of the Tribulation, will join with the Lord and participate in the battle to reclaim the world for the rule of Christ.

The saints are not the only ones who will comprise the army of the Lord. "When the Son of Man comes in His glory, and all the holy angels with Him, then He will sit on the throne of His glory" (Matthew 25:31).

In Revelation 5:11, John tells us, "I heard the voice of many angels around the throne, the living creatures, and the elders; and the number of them was ten thousand times ten thousand, and thousands of thousands." The Greek says literally, "numbering myriads of myriads and thousands of thousands."

This mixture of saints and angels calls to mind scenes from great fantasies such as *The Chronicles of Narnia* and *The Lord of the Rings*, where humans fight alongside other-worldly creatures to defeat the forces of evil. It's a thrilling picture to think of human saints side-by-side with God's angels in battle.

REMEMBER: When Jesus entered Jerusalem on Palm Sunday, He came humbly, riding on the foal of a donkey. But when He returns, it will be with might and power, atop a war horse. The Day of Reckoning will have come at last!

TAKE TWO!

Prophetic Connection: *God's Word gives us confidence regarding the Second Coming of Christ in part because of how accurate it was regarding His first advent.*

The Second Coming of Christ is a central theme of much of the Bible, and it is one of the best-attested promises in all of Scripture. Christians can rest in the sure conviction that, just as Jesus came to earth the first time, so He will return at the conclusion of the Great Tribulation.

As Christians, we are quite familiar with our Lord's first coming to earth because we accept the record of the four Gospels. It is history. In a similar way, the Bible clearly tells us that He is coming to earth again. Though the exact expression "the Second Coming of Christ" is not found in the Bible, Scripture makes the assertion in many places. For example, the writer of Hebrews tells us, "And as it is appointed for men to die once, but after this the judgment, so Christ was offered once to bear the sins of many. To those who eagerly wait for Him He will appear *a second time*, apart from sin, for salvation" (9:27–28, emphasis added).

However, the Old Testament prophecies of Christ's first and second comings are so mingled that Jewish scholars did not clearly see them as separate events. Their perception of these prophecies was like viewing a mountain range from a distance. They saw what appeared to be one mountain, failing to see that there was another equally high mountain behind it, obscured from their sight through the perspective of distance. The prophets saw both comings of Christ either as one event or as very closely related in time.

This mixing of two prophetic events into one may partially explain why the Jews as a whole rejected Christ. The prophecies speak of the Messiah both enduring great suffering and accomplishing a great conquest. They thought the suffering savior would become the conquering savior in one advent. They did not realize He would come a first time to suffer and then a second time to conquer.

It is evident that even Jesus' first disciples expected Him to fulfill the glorious promises relating to His Second Coming when He appeared the first time. Only after He ascended to heaven did they realize that they were living in the time period between His two appearances, as if on a plain between two mountains.

REMEMBER: "Heaven must receive him until the time comes for God to restore everything, as he promised long ago through his holy prophets" (Acts 3:21 NIV).

EVERY EYE WILL SEE HIM

Prophetic Connection: *The Bible has much more to say about Jesus' Second Coming than about His first incarnation in our world.*

Although Christians are most familiar with the first coming of Christ, it is the Second Coming that gets the most ink in the Bible. References to the Second Coming outnumber references to the first by a factor of eight to one. Scholars count 1,845 biblical references to the Second Coming, including 318 in the New Testament.

While many of the Old Testament prophets wrote concerning the Second Coming of Christ, it is Zechariah who has given us the clearest and most concise prediction of it:

> Then the LORD will go forth and fight against those nations, as He fights in the day of battle. And in that day His feet will stand on the Mount of Olives, which faces Jerusalem on the east. (14:3–4)

Centuries later, Jesus was speaking from the Mount of Olives when He affirmed His Second Coming to His disciples in dramatic and cataclysmic terms: "The sign of the Son of Man will appear in heaven, and then all the tribes of the earth will mourn, and they will see the Son of Man coming on the clouds of heaven with power and great glory" (Matthew 24:30).

Immediately following Christ's ascension into heaven, two angels appeared to the stunned disciples and spoke words of comfort to them. "Men of Galilee," they said, "why do you stand gazing up into heaven? This same Jesus, who was taken up from you into heaven, will so come in like manner as you saw Him go into heaven" (Acts 1:11). Jesus ascended to heaven from the Mount of Olives. According to the angels, Christ will return to that very same spot—the Mount of Olives—just as Zechariah foretold.

In the first chapter of Revelation, John records, "Behold, He is coming with clouds, and every eye will see Him, even they who pierced Him. And all the tribes of the earth will mourn because of Him" (v. 7). And in the last chapter—indeed, almost the last words of the New Testament—our Lord emphatically affirms His Second Coming: "He who testifies to these things says, 'Surely I am coming quickly.' Amen. Even so, come, Lord Jesus!" (22:20).

Obviously, we have excellent reason to anticipate the return of Christ. The Bible affirms it throughout as a certainty, describing it in specific terms and with ample corroboration.

REMEMBER: "And then the lawless one will be revealed, whom the Lord will consume with the breath of His mouth and destroy with the brightness of His coming" (2 Thessalonians 2:8).

117

A STELLAR EVENT. CELESTIAL. COSMIC.

Prophetic Connection: *From the moment Christ's feet touch the ground on our world once more, nothing will ever be the same again.*

Twice in the book of Revelation we are told that the door to heaven will be opened. It is first opened to receive the church into heaven at the time of the Rapture: "After these things I looked, and behold, a door standing open in heaven. And the first voice which I heard was like a trumpet speaking with me, saying, 'Come up here, and I will show you things which must take place after this'" (4:1). The door swings open a second time for Christ and His church to proceed from heaven on their militant march back to earth (19:11, 14). The first opening is for the Rapture of the saints; the second is for the return of Christ!

When Jesus arrives on earth the second time, His landing will dramatically herald the purpose of His coming. The moment His feet touch the Mount of Olives, that mountain will split apart, creating a broad passageway from Jerusalem to Jericho: "On that day his feet will stand on the Mount of Olives, east of Jerusalem. And the Mount of Olives will split apart, making a wide valley running from east to west. Half the mountain will move toward the north and half toward the south" (Zechariah 14:4). As you can imagine, this will be an unprecedented geological cataclysm. In describing it, Dr. Tim LaHaye wrote: "There will be a Stellar Event. Celestial. Cosmic. Greater than earth. Greater than the heavens. And it will suck the air out of humanity's lungs and send men and women and kings and presidents and tyrants to their knees. It will have no need of spotlights, fog machines, amplified music, synthesizers, or special effects. It will be real."[1]

Thus Christ's return will be amplified by a devastating spectacle that will make Hollywood disaster movies look like Saturday morning child's fare. The world will see and recognize its rightful Lord and King. Whereas He came the first time in humility and simplicity, this time His glory and majesty will be spectacularly displayed for all to see. To put it another way, the first time Jesus came to earth, He was unrecognized by many; the second time He comes, no one will doubt who He is.

REMEMBER: The term *apocalypse* means "unveiling," and when Jesus returns, the veil will be lifted. All those who doubted Him and refused to believe will finally know the truth.

BEHOLD THE RIDER ON A WHITE HORSE

Prophetic Connection: *The three titles ascribed to Christ in Revelation 19 offer important insight into His role at the end times.*

In Revelation 19, the descending Lord is given three meaningful titles.

> Now I saw heaven opened, and behold, a white horse. And He who sat on him was called Faithful and True, and in righteousness He judges and makes war. . . . He had a name written that no one knew except Himself . . . and His name is called The Word of God. . . . And He has on His robe and on His thigh a name written: KING OF KINGS AND LORD OF LORDS. (vv. 11–13, 16)

These three names are not merely rhetorical embellishments or empty titles—as if such false labels could be applied to the conquering Christ in Scripture! Prophecy scholar Harry Ironside gives us insight into the significance of these names:

> In these three names we have set forth first, our Lord's dignity as the Eternal Son; second, His incarnation—the Word became Flesh; and last, His second advent to reign as King of Kings and Lord of Lords.[1]

These three names encompass the entire ministry of the Lord Jesus Christ. The first name, the mysterious one known only to God, indicates His intimacy and oneness with the Father and thus His eternal existence, including His role in the Trinity as creator and sustainer of the world.

The second name, the Word of God, harks back to the first chapter of John's gospel and indicates His incarnation when "the Word became flesh" (v. 14), walked as a man upon this earth, and revealed God to us.

The third name, the majestic and towering syllables "King of kings and Lord of lords," is the title He will wear at His Second Coming, designating His role as the sovereign ruler over all the earth. He alone is worthy. He alone is due all glory and honor and blessing. And at His coming, the entire world will know.

REMEMBER: Christ's return will not merely be the end of history as we know it; it will also mark the beginning of a new age and "the renewal of all things" (Matthew 19:28 NIV).

THE SPLENDOR OF THE KING

Prophetic Connection: *Scripture offers a compelling portrait of Christ's return at the Second Coming.*

When Jesus returns to earth, it will not be as the inconspicuous carpenter people saw during His earthly ministry. Instead, He will come in all His glory—and His appearance will speak volumes.

In the book of Revelation, *the eyes* of the returning Christ are described as burning like a flame of fire, signifying His ability as a judge to see deeply into the hearts of men and ferret out all injustice (1:14; 2:18; 19:12). His eyes will pierce through the motives of nations and individuals and judge them for what they really are, not for how they hope their masks of hypocrisy will make them appear!

The head of the returning Christ is crowned with many crowns (19:12), testifying to His status as the absolute sovereign King of kings and Lord of lords—the undisputed monarch of the entire earth. Famed nineteenth-century London preacher Charles Haddon Spurgeon described the comfort and security that we derive from the sovereignty of Christ:

I am sure there is no more delightful doctrine to a Christian, than that of Christ's absolute sovereignty. I am glad there is no such thing as chance, that nothing is left to itself, but that Christ everywhere hath sway. If I thought that there was a devil in hell that Christ did not govern, I should be afraid that devil would destroy me. If I thought there was a circumstance on earth, which Christ did not over-rule, I should fear that that circumstance would ruin me. Nay, if there were an angel in heaven that was not one of Jehovah's subjects, I should tremble even at him. But since Christ is King of kings, and I am his poor brother, one whom he loves, I give all my cares to him, for he careth for me; and leaning on his breast, my soul hath full repose, confidence, and security.[1]

The robe of the returning Christ is dipped in blood, reminding us that He is the sacrificial Lamb of God. John described King Jesus as "the Lamb slain from the foundation of the world" (13:8). In fact, Jesus will be represented to us as the Lamb of God throughout eternity. In a sense, eternity will be an extended communion service as we remember forever with love and gratitude the sacrifice of Jesus Christ that united us with God and gave us an eternity of joy with Him.

REMEMBER: "The Son is the radiance of God's glory and the exact representation of his being" (Hebrews 1:3 NIV).

A DAY OF JUDGMENT

Prophetic Connection: *The end of the Tribulation will initiate a time of justice and judgment the likes of which the world has never seen.*

When Jesus returns to this earth to put down the world's ultimate rebellion, the armies of heaven will accompany Him. John described these armies as "clothed in fine linen, white and clean, [following] Him on white horses" (Revelation 19:14). In the short epistle that immediately precedes the book of Revelation, Jude described this epic event:

> Now Enoch, the seventh from Adam, prophesied about these men also, saying, "Behold, the Lord comes with ten thousands of His saints, to execute judgment on all, to convict all who are ungodly among them of all their ungodly deeds which they have committed in an ungodly way, and of all the harsh things which ungodly sinners have spoken against Him." (vv. 14–15)

In one short verse, Jude used the word *ungodly* four times. This repetition is not accidental. Jude was emphasizing the fact that when Christ comes the second time,

His long-suffering patience will have run its course. He will come to impose judgment upon those who have defied Him, and that judgment will be massive. In His loving mercy, God endeavored to turn sinful people away from their fatal rebellion. But the people in the last days will have hardened their hearts beyond repentance.

In his second letter to the Thessalonians, Paul wrote in chilling terms of the judgment that will descend on these rebels:

> These shall be punished with everlasting destruction from the presence of the Lord and from the glory of His power, when He comes, in that Day, to be glorified in His saints and to be admired among all those who believe, because our testimony among you was believed. (1:9–10)

As we have seen, the armies of heaven that accompany Christ in His Second Coming will be made up of saints and angels—people like you and me standing side-by-side with heavenly beings of immense power. These legions are dressed not in military fatigues but in dazzling white. Yet they need not worry about their pristine uniforms getting soiled because their role will be largely ceremonial and honorary; they will not fight. Jesus Himself will slay the rebels with the deadly sword darting out of His mouth.

REMEMBER: "Kiss the Son, lest He be angry, and you perish in the way, when His wrath is kindled but a little. Blessed are all those who put their trust in Him" (Psalm 2:12).

A FIERY FATE

Prophetic Connection: *The Bible reveals the ultimate end for the Antichrist and those who serve him.*

The Tribulation will be a time of worldwide rebellion against God, largely spurred by two satanic figures: the Antichrist (the beast) and the false prophet. What will happen to those two after the Tribulation? The Bible tells us that God simply snatches them up and flings them into the fiery lake. "Then the beast was captured, and with him the false prophet who worked signs in his presence, by which he deceived those who received the mark of the beast and those who worshiped his image. These two were cast alive into the lake of fire burning with brimstone" (Revelation 19:20).

These two evil creatures have the unwanted honor of actually getting to that awful place before Satan, whose confinement occurs much later: "The devil, who deceived them, was cast into the lake of fire and brimstone where the beast and false prophet are. And they will be tormented day and night forever and ever" (Revelation 20:10). Satan does not join the beast and the false prophet there until the end of the Millennium, one thousand years later.

Harry Ironside offers an interesting sidelight concerning

the nature of the punishment these two men experience: "'Note that two men, are taken alive'. . . . These two men are 'cast alive into [the lake burning with fire and brimstone]' where a thousand years later, they are still said to be 'suffering the vengeance of eternal fire' (Jude 7)." Ironside focuses our attention on two important truths from God's Word; the men are alive when they arrive, and they are still alive a thousand years later—and still experiencing suffering. He draws a profound conclusion: "the lake of fire is neither annihilation nor purgatorial because it neither annihilates nor purifies these two fallen foes of God and man after a thousand years under judgment."[1]

As God's judgment in Revelation clearly shows, God is not soft. He intends to remake us in His own image, which is often a painful and self-denying process. If we refuse to be remade, we must endure the hellish consequence that choice brings. As John's vision shows us, hell is frightfully real. And it shows how deadly it is to be an enemy of the almighty God. His power is infinite, and His justice is certain. No rebellion can stand against Him, and the consequences of such rebellion are terrible and eternal.

REMEMBER: "Do not be deceived, God is not mocked; for whatever a man sows, that he will also reap" (Galatians 6:7).

LIVING IN LIGHT OF PROPHECY

Prophetic Connection: *Biblical prophecy is a clear lens through which we can view the events of our world—and find truth.*

There are few subjects more relevant today than biblical prophecy. In fact, as we move into times that are so clearly depicted in the prophetic Scriptures, many people are looking at today's headlines and asking, "What in the world is going on?" I cannot imagine how people of faith live in today's cataclysmic world without using the Word of God to gain the proper perspective on world events.

In spite of the high value inherent in understanding future events for their own sake, studying prophecy has an even higher and more practical value for followers of Jesus. It provides a compelling motivation for living the Christian life. The immediacy of prophetic events shows the need to live each moment in Christlike readiness.

As revered Southern Baptist evangelist Vance Havner has put it, "The devil has chloroformed the atmosphere of this age." Therefore, in view of the sure promises of Christ's return, as believers, we are to do more than merely be ready;

we are to be expectant. In our day of "anarchy, apostasy, and apathy," Havner suggests that expectant living means: "we need to take down our 'Do Not Disturb' signs . . . snap out of our stupor and come out of our coma and awake from our apathy."[1] Havner reminds us that God's Word calls to us to awake out of our sleep, and to walk in righteousness, in the light Christ gives us (Romans 13:11; 1 Corinthians 15:34; Ephesians 5:14). Prophecy can provide the wake-up call that Dr. Havner calls for.

When we have heard and understood the truth of Christ's promised return, we cannot just keep living our lives in the same old way. Future events have present implications that we cannot ignore. When we know that Christ is coming again to this earth, we cannot go on being the same people. However, as we anticipate Jesus's return, we are not to foolishly set dates and leave our jobs and homes to wait for Him on some mountain. Instead, we are to remain busy doing the work set before us, living in love and serving in ministry, even when the days grow dark and the nights long.

Be encouraged! Be anticipating! We are secure; we belong to Christ. And as the old gospel song says, "Soon and very soon, we are going to see the King!"

REMEMBER: Jesus testified, "And behold, I am coming quickly, and My reward is with Me, to give to every one according to his work. I am the Alpha and the Omega, the Beginning and the End, the First and the Last" (Revelation 22:12–13).

NOTES

DAY 1

1. Romesh Ratnesae, "May 14, 1948," *Time*, http://www.time.com/time/magazine/article/0,9171,1004510,00.html (accessed February 27, 2008).
2. The Declaration of Independence (Israel), 14 May 1948, Israel Ministry of Foreign Affairs, "The Signatories of the Declaration of the Establishment of the State of Israel," http://www.mfa.gov.il/mfa/history/modern%20history/israel%20at%2050/the%20signatories%20of%20the%20declaration%20of%20the%20establis (accessed February 25, 2008).

DAY 4

1. John Walvoord, "Will Israel Possess the Promised Land?" *Jesus the King Is Coming*, Charles Lee Feinberg, ed. (Chicago: Moody Press, 1975), 128.

DAY 5

1. Joel C. Rosenberg, from the audio track of the DVD *Epicenter* (Carol Stream, IL: Tyndale House Publishers, Inc., 2007). Used with permission.

DAY 7

1. Paul Crespo, "Author: 'Something Is Going on Between Russia and Iran,'" Newsmax, January 30, 2007, http://archive.newsmax.com/archives/articles/2007/1/29/212432.shtml?s=1h (accessed March 26, 2008).
2. Joel C. Rosenberg, *Epicenter* (Carol Stream, IL: Tyndale House Publishers, 2006), 113.

DAY 9

1. "The Mists of Time," Amazing Discoveries, http://amazingdiscoveries.org/the-mists-oftime.html (accessed March 21, 2008).

DAY 11

1. Arno Froese, *How Democracy Will Elect the Antichrist* (Columbia, SC: Olive Press, 1997), 165.
2. Quoted in David L. Larsen, *Telling the Old, Old Story: The Art of Narrative Preaching* (Grand Rapids, MI: Kregel, 1995), 214.

DAY 12

1. "Ahmadinejad's 2005 address to the United Nations," Wikisource: United Nations, http://en.wikisource.org/wiki/Ahmadinejad's_2005_address_to_the_United-Nations.
2. John F. Walvoord and Mark Hitchcock, *Armageddon, Oil, and Terror* (Carol Stream, IL: Tyndale House Publishers, 2007), 44.

DAY 13

1. "A Testimony from a Saudi Believer," *Answering Islam: A Christian-Muslim Dialog and Apologetic*, http://answering-islam.org./Testimonies/saudi.html (accessed April 20, 2006).

DAY 14

1. *Merriam-Webster Online*, s. v. "rapture," www.merriam-webster.com/dictionary
   /rapture (accessed June 5, 2008).

DAY 21

1. Adapted from Newt Gingrich, *Rediscovering God in America* (Nashville, TN:
   Integrity, 2006), 130.
2. "President's Proclamation," *The New York Times*, November 21, 1982, http://select
   .nytimes.com/search/restricted/article?res=F30611FB395DOC728EDDA80994
   (accessed April 15, 2008).
3. "Washington's First Inauguration Address, April 30, 1789," Library of Congress,
   www.loc.gov/exhibits/treasures/trt051.html (accessed June 5, 2008).

DAY 22

1. John F. Walvoord, "America and the Cause of World Missions," *America in History
   and Bible Prophecy*, Thomas McCall, ed. (Chicago: Moody Press, 1976), 21.
2. Gordon Robertson, "Into All the World," Christian Broadcasting Network,
   http://www.cbn.com/spirituallife/churchandministry/churchhistory/Gordon
   _Into_World.aspx (accessed November 1, 2007).
3. Luis Bush, "Where Are We Now?" Mission Frontiers, 2003, http://www
   .missionfrontiers.org/2000/03/bts20003.htm (accessed November 1, 2007).

DAY 23

1. Mark Hitchcock, *America in the End Times*, newsletter, The Left Behind Prophecy
   Club.
2. Herman A. Hoyt, *Is the United States in Prophecy?* (Winona Lake, IN: BMH Books,
   1977), 16.

DAY 24

1. Vance Havner, *In Times Like These* (Old Tappan, NJ: Fleming H. Revell, 1969), 21.

DAY 29

1. Arthur W. Pink, *The Antichrist* (Minneapolis: Klich & Klich, 1979), 77.

DAY 30

1. Charles Colson, *Kingdoms in Conflict* (Grand Rapids, MI: Zondervan, 1987), 68.

DAY 31

1. W. A. Criswell, *Expository Sermons on Revelation*, vol. IV (Dallas: Criswell
   Publishing, 1995), 109.

DAY 33

1. "President Delivers State of the Union Address," press release dated January 29,
   2002, The White House, http://www.whitehouse.gov/news
   /releases/2002/01/20020129-11. html (accessed March 10, 2008).

DAY 34

1. John F. Walvoord, *The Nations in Prophecy* (Grand Rapids, MI: Zondervan,
   1978), 107.
2. Erik Hildinger, *Warriors of the Steppe: A Military History of Central Asia, 500* B.C.
   to 1700 (New York: DaCapo Press, 2001), 33.

DAY 35

1. Walvoord, *The Nations in Prophecy*, 106.
2. Walvoord, 101.
3. Edward Lucas, "The New Cold War," www.edwardlucas.com (accessed June 6, 2008).

DAY 36

1. "Iran," CIA-The World Factbook, https://www.cia.gov/library/publications /the-worldfactbook/geos/ir.html (accessed June 26, 2008).
2. Nazila Fathi, "Iran's President Says 'Israel Must Be Wiped Off the Map,'" *The New York Times*, October 26, 2007, http://www.nytimes.com/2005/10 /26/international/middleeast/26cnd-iran.html (accessed April 18, 2008).
3. Aaron Klein, "Hezbollah: Rockets fired into Israel directed by Iran," WorldNetDaily, May 7, 2007, http://www.worldnetdaily.com/news/article .asp?ARTICLE_ID=55572 (accessed September 5, 2007).

DAY 37

1. Edward Gibbon, *The Decline and Fall of the Roman Empire* (London: Milman Co., London, n.d.), 1:204.

DAY 38

1. David L. Cooper, *When Gog's Armies Meet the Almighty* (Los Angeles, CA: The Biblical Research Society, 1958), 17.
2. Theodore Epp, *Russia's Doom Prophesied* (Lincoln, NE: Good News Broadcasting, 1954), 40–42.

DAY 40

1. Amir Mizroch, "Israel launches new push to reduce its oil dependency," *Jerusalem Post*, September 27, 2007, posted at Forecast Highs, http:// forecasthighs.wordpress.com/2007/09/27/ Israel-launches-new-push-to -reduce-its-oil-dependency (accessed October 2, 2007).
2. Nazila Fathi, "Mideast Turmoil: Tehran; Iranian Urges Muslims to Use Oil as a Weapon," *The New York Times*, April 6, 2002, http://query.nytimes.com/gst /fullpage.html?res=9A05E5D6173DF935A35757C0A9649C8B63&scp =3&sq=Nazila+Fathi&st=nyt (accessed June 25, 2008).
3. "Israel GDP per Capita," CEIC, https://www.ceicdata.com/en/indicator/israel /gdp-per-capita (accessed January 7, 2025).

DAY 41

1. H. D. M. Spence and Joseph Excell, eds., *The Pulpit Commentary*, vol. 28 (New York: Funk & Wagnalls, 1880–93), 298.

DAY 46

1. Vernon J. McGee, *Through the Bible*, vol. 3 (Nashville, TN: Thomas Nelson, Inc., 1982), 513.

DAY 49

1. John Walvoord and Mark Hitchcock, *Armageddon, Oil, and Terror*, 174.

DAY 50

1. John F. Walvoord, "The Way of the Kings of the East," *Light for the World's Darkness*, John W. Bradbury, ed. (New York: Loizeaux Brothers, 1944), 164.

DAY 51

    1. A. Sims, ed., *The Coming Great War* (Toronto: A. Sims, Publisher, 1932), 12–13.

DAY 55

    1. Tim LaHaye, *The Rapture*, 89.

DAY 56

    1. Harry A. Ironside, *Revelation* (Grand Rapids, MI: Kregel, 2004), 187–188.

DAY 57

    1. Charles Spurgeon, "The Saviour's Many Crowns," a sermon (no. 281) delivered October 30, 1859, *The Spurgeon Archive*, accessed June 7, 2008, www.spurgeon .org/sermons/0281.htm.

DAY 59

    1. Ironside, *Revelation*, 189-190.

DAY 60

    1. Vance Havner, *In Times Like These* (Old Tappan, NJ: Fleming H. Revell Company, 1969), 29.

ABOUT THE AUTHOR

DAVID JEREMIAH is the founder of Turning Point, an international ministry committed to providing Christians with sound Bible teaching through radio and television, the internet, live events, resource materials, and books. He is the author of more than fifty books, including *Forward*, *Overcomer*, *A Life Beyond Amazing*, *Airship Genesis: Kids Study Bible*, and *The Jeremiah Study Bible*.

Dr. Jeremiah serves as the senior pastor of Shadow Mountain Community Church in El Cajon, California, where he resides with his wife, Donna. They have four grown children, twelve grandchildren, and one great-grandchild. Learn more at DavidJeremiah.org.